CHAMPIONS OF FREEDOM

The Ludwig von Mises Lecture Series

CHAMPIONS OF FREEDOM
Volume 25

BETWEEN POWER AND LIBERTY
ECONOMICS AND THE LAW

Richard M. Ebeling, Executive Editor

Lissa Roche, General Editor

Hillsdale College Press
Hillsdale, Michigan 49242

Hillsdale College Press

Books by the Hillsdale College Press include The Christian Vision series; Champions of Freedom series; and other works.

The views expressed in this volume are not necessarily the views of Hillsdale College.

The Champions of Freedom series
BETWEEN POWER AND LIBERTY:
ECONOMICS AND THE LAW
©1998 Hillsdale College Press, Hillsdale, Michigan 49242

Printed in the United States of America

Photo: Douglas Coon

First printing 1998

Library of Congress Catalog Card Number 97-074610
ISBN 0-916308-63-4

Contents

Contributors

SPENCER ABRAHAM was elected to the United States Senate in 1994. He is the first Michigan Republican to win a Senate seat since 1978. A member of the Judiciary, Commerce, and Budget Committees, he was named chairman of the Judiciary Subcommittee on Immigration and the Commerce Subcommittee on Manufacturing and Competitiveness during the 105th Congress.

Senator Abraham graduated from Harvard Law School in 1979. He taught at Thomas M. Cooley Law School and joined the Detroit firm of Miller, Canfield, Paddock and Stone. In 1982, he co-founded the Federalist Society for Law and Public Policy Studies. That same year, at age thirty, he became the youngest chairman of the Michigan Republican Party. In 1990, he was appointed the White House deputy chief of staff for the Office of the Vice President. He also served for a time as the co-chairman of the National Republican Congressional Committee. Today, he is one of the most high-profile leaders of the Senate, the subject and the author of numerous articles in the national press.

CLINT BOLICK serves as vice president and director of litigation at the Institute for Justice, which he helped found in 1991. The Institute is devoted to constitutional litigation protecting individual liberty and challenging the regulatory welfare states. It fulfills this mission by teaching public interest litigation skills to lawyers, law students, and policy activists. Mr. Bolick is also engaged in cutting-edge cases around the nation, defending school choice programs, challenging barriers to entrepreneurship, and upholding such proposals as the recent California Civil Rights Initiative. Earlier this year, *American Lawyer* selected him as one of the nation's top forty-five young lawyers "whose vision and commitment are changing lives." He is the author of *Affirmative Action Fraud: Can We Restore the American Civil Rights Vision?* and *Grassroots Tyranny: The Limits of Federalism.* He received his law degree from the University of California-Davis.

JOSEPH BROADUS is a professor of law at George Mason University. Before joining the faculty, he was counsel to the Florida House Committee on Retirement Personnel and Collective Bargaining; a special assistant to a member of the U.S. Civil Rights Commission; and a research associate at the Center for Employment Relations and the Law. He has been a guest on the *McNeil-Lehrer NewsHour,* C-Span, National Empowerment Television, and many other news programs and networks.

A former reporter for the *Miami Herald,* his commentary has also been featured in the *ABA Journal,* the *Civil Rights Law Journal,* the *Hartford Courant,* the *Labor Law Journal,* the *National Black Law Review,* the *Washington Times,* and the *World and I.* Professor Broadus has contributed to three books: *Actions and Remedies; Law, Economics, and Civil Justice Reform;* and *Black and Right.* He is currently at work on a book of his own critically examining the legal and societal impact of same-sex marriage. He holds a J.D. degree from Florida State University.

HARRY BROWNE is one of the nation's top investment advisors, the author of nine books, a well-known radio and television personality, and the 1996 Libertarian Party candidate for President of the United States. He rose to prominence in 1970 when his book, *How You Can Profit from the Coming Devaluation,* made the *New York Times* best-seller list. The sequel, *You Can Profit from a Monetary Crisis,* not only made the list but remained on it for thirty-nine weeks, reaching the number-one spot as the best-selling book in America. He has written six more investment books, including another best-seller. His books have sold more than two million copies.

Since 1974, Mr. Browne has been writing *Harry Browne's Special Reports,* a financial newsletter for investors. He has made numerous appearances on CNN, *Larry King,* CNBC, and various network television programs. He also delivers a daily five-minute radio commentary that is aired on over six hundred stations.

RICHARD M. EBELING is the Ludwig von Mises Professor of Economics at Hillsdale College. A former professor at the University of Dallas, he joined the Hillsdale faculty in 1988. In addition, he serves on the editorial board of the *Review of Austrian Economics* and as vice president of the Future of Freedom Foundation. He has edited *Money, Method, and the Market Process: Essays by Ludwig von Mises* and a number of volumes in the Hillsdale College Press Champions of Freedom series. He is co-editor of *The Dangers of Socialized Medicine.*

    Professor Ebeling has lectured extensively on privatization and monetary reform throughout the United States, Latin America, and the former Soviet Union, where he has consulted with the Lithuanian government, the city of Moscow, and the Russian parliament. He is working on a biography of Ludwig von Mises.

ROBERT L. FORMAINI has had a diverse career. After earning a bachelor's degree in music from Ithaca College in New York, he served for two years in the U. S. Army. Then he taught in the Virginia public school system and played in the Richmond Symphony Orchestra. But a lifelong interest in public policy led him to move to California to join the then newly founded think tank, the Cato Institute, as vice president and editor of the *Cato Journal.* He went on to earn a Ph.D. in political economy from the University of Texas and to teach at such schools as Reinhardt College, Oxford College of Emory University, and the University of Dallas. Dr. Formaini also helped found, and served as executive director of, the National Center for Policy Analysis in Dallas. Currently, he is a senior economist and public policy advisor at the Federal Reserve Bank in Dallas.

BETTINA BIEN GREAVES' first job was with the Foreign Economic Administration during World War II; she served in Bolivia and Austria. By the war's end she had become disillusioned with bureaucracy and was convinced that the solution to international conflicts rested on internal trade. Her serious study of economics and of the free market economy started in 1947, when she worked for the short-lived Foundation for Freedom in Washington, D.C. She came to the Foundation for Economic Education (FEE) in 1951. That same year, she began attending the graduate seminar in economic theory taught by Professor Ludwig von Mises at New York University. She continued as a regular seminar participant for eighteen years, until Mises retired in 1969. After his death she translated a number of his German monographs, which appeared in English as *On the Manipulation of Money and Credit.*

Mrs. Greaves is still a resident scholar at FEE and a contributing editor to its monthly journal, *The Freeman.* She is the author of *Free Market Economics: A Basic Reader,* a contributor to *The Wisdom of Henry Hazlitt* and *Toward Liberty,* and editor of such works as *Economic Freedom and Free Enterprise* and *Austrian Economics: An Anthology.* She holds a master's degree in library science from Columbia University.

STEPHEN MOORE is the director of fiscal policy studies at the Cato Institute, a free market think tank now based in Washington, D.C. Prior to joining Cato, he worked as a senior economist at the joint Economic Committee, advising Representative Dick Armey of Texas on budget, tax, and competitiveness issues, and helping to write the famous Armey flat tax proposal. Mr. Moore has also served as the Grover M. Hermann Fellow in budgetary affairs at the Heritage Foundation, as a special consultant to the National Economic Commission, and as research director of President Reagan's Commission on Privatization.

Currently he is an editor for *National Review* and a frequent contributor to the *Wall Street Journal, Human Events,* and *Reader's Digest.* He also appears on such television shows as PBS's *NewsHour with Jim Lehrer,* CNN's *Money Line,* NBC's *Nightly News,* Fox's *Morning News,* and the *McLaughlin Group.* And he has written three books: *Privatization: A Strategy for Taming the Deficit Economy; Still an Open Door? U.S. Immigration Policy and the American Economy;* and *Government: America's #1 Growth Industry.* Mr. Moore holds an M.A. in economics from George Mason University.

WILLIAM "BILLY" S. MORRIS, III, is chairman and CEO of the Morris Communications Corporation, which is headquartered in Augusta and which publishes thirty-two daily and ten other newspapers throughout the country, as well as several magazines in Georgia. Its other divisions include printing, radio, outdoor advertising, and computer services. Mr. Morris also serves on the boards of numerous organizations, including the Newspaper Association of America, New Directions for News, Paine College, Columbia Theological Seminary, the Greater Augusta Sports Council, the Morris Museum of Art, and the Atlantic Coast Cutting Horse Association. In addition, he founded and currently chairs the Augusta Futurity and is CEO of the National Barrel Horse Association. He holds a B.A. in journalism from the University of Georgia.

GEORGE ROCHE has served as president of Hillsdale College since 1971. Formerly the presidentially appointed chairman of the National Council on Educational Research, the director of seminars at the Foundation for Economic Education, a professor of history at the Colorado School of Mines, and a U.S. Marine, he is the author of twelve books, including five Conservative Book Club selections. His latest book is *The Fall of the Ivory Tower: Government Funding, Corruption, and the Bankrupting of American Higher Education* (Regnery Publishing, 1994). Reviews and excerpts of this latest volume have appeared in many sources, including *Forbes,* the *Wall Street Journal,* and *Reader's Digest.* It was also the subject of a cover story in a 1994 issue of *Insight* magazine as "Book of the Year." *L.A. Times* syndicated columnist Cal Thomas has called it "the most important book on higher education since *The Closing of the American Mind.*"

BERNARD H. SIEGAN is a graduate of the University of Chicago Law School and has been distinguished professor of law at the University of San Diego Law School since 1975. He is the author of more than fifty articles and has written or edited eleven books. The most widely cited are: *Land Use Without Zoning; Other People's Property; Economic Liberties and the Constitution;* and *The Supreme Court's Constitution—An Inquiry into Judicial Review and Its Impact on Society. Drafting a Constitution for a Nation or Republic Emerging into Freedom* has been translated into Spanish, Portuguese, Polish, and Russian.

Professor Siegan has served as a member of the National Commission on the Bicentennial of the Constitution (established by the U.S. Congress), as a member of President Reagan's Commission on Housing, and as a consultant to three federal agencies: the Department of Justice, the Department of Housing and Urban Development, and the Federal Trade Commission. As one of the nation's leading constitutional experts he has also been a consultant for governments and private groups in Argentina, Armenia, Bolivia, Brazil, Bulgaria, Canada, Czechoslovakia, Peru, Poland, Tajikistan, and Ukraine.

GAYLORD K. SWIM is president of Swim Investment Management in Orem, Utah. He is also chairman of the board of directors of the EFI Electronics Corporation in Salt Lake City. Although he is a prominent business leader in his community, his most outstanding achievements are in the area of philanthropy. He is founder and chairman of the Sutherland Institute, an awards committee member for America's Freedom Festival at Provo, chairman and trustee of the American Heritage Schools, and chairman and trustee of the Rural Health Management Corporation.

In the past, Mr. Swim has also served as a board member for the Deseret Foundation, the Covey Leadership Center, the Boy Scouts of America, and the Central Valley Medical Center, and as an advisor to the Smith Center for Free Enterprise at Brigham Young University. In addition, he is the author of a nationally distributed guide called *Discovering Charity* for the Philanthropy Roundtable, as well as a number of articles for such publications as *Philanthropy, Investor's Guide, Utah Business,* and *Financial Insights.* He received a master's degree in political science from Brigham Young University.

Foreword

For twenty-five years, America's most distinguished scholars and active decisionmakers have met on the Hillsdale College campus to pay homage to one of the world's greatest champions of freedom, Austrian School economist Ludwig von Mises (1881–1973). Perhaps the College's proudest possession is Mises' personal library. Upon bequeathing his library to us, Professor Mises said he had done so because "Hillsdale, more than any other educational institution, most strongly represents the free market ideas to which I have given my life."

When the history of the twentieth century is written, the Mises name will surely be remembered as that of the foremost economist of our age. Certainly the history of one period during this century ought to include his name writ large: the one in which we are now living, the one that will be forever remembered as the time when the Berlin Wall finally came crashing down. The man who took out the first brick was Ludwig von Mises. He did it with books such as *The Theory of Money and Credit, The Free and Prosperous Commonwealth, Omnipotent Government, Bureaucracy,* and *Human Action.*

Mises based his theory of economics on the supremacy of the individual. The rational, purposeful, day-to-day decisions of ordinary men and women are what constitute the market and are the basis of all human action. It was his understanding of the market as a process, against the background of continually changing conditions and limited individual knowledge, that set his theory so clearly apart from the rigid, mathematical attempts of other economists bent on devising "models" of equilibrium.

Few economists perceived so clearly the consequences of the ideas set in motion by the statist and collectivist mentality. He warned that the greatest danger to Western society would come with the increasing concentration of political and economic power in the hands of the state. He used the example of communism in the Soviet Union and Eastern Europe to point out that the peril was real indeed.

It was Mises who wrote so eloquently and forcefully that the state could never successfully control the marketplace any more than it could control the lives of men. In fact, Mises' testimony finally convinced prominent Marxist-Leninist intellectuals to admit in the 1980s, "The world is run by human action, not by human design."

This twenty-fifth volume of the Champions of Freedom series is based on the same premise, and it explores the future of American business in the context of Mises' important and enduring intellectual legacy.

GEORGE ROCHE
President
Hillsdale College

Introduction

> The legal inviolability of property is obviously a mere
> mockery, where the sovereign power is unable to make
> the laws respected, where it either practices robbery
> itself, or is impotent to repress it in others; or where
> possession is rendered perpetually insecure, by the
> intricacy of legislative enactments, and the subtleties of
> technical nicety. Nor can property be said to exist, where
> it is not a matter of reality as well as of right.
>
> Jean-Baptiste Say
A Treatise on Political Economy[1]

When the classical economists of the nineteenth century explained
the negative effects of government regulation and control over
economic activity, they would sometimes point to extreme cases in
which the state possessed wide or even complete arbitrary power
over the wealth of their subjects. For example, the famous English
economist Nassau W. Senior recounted his observations during a journey he made to the Turkish Empire in the Middle East
during the 1850s. While in Egypt a local businessman told Senior:

> The calamity of this country, as of every oriental despotism is
> insecurity. Nothing that I possess is really mine. I have a house,
> the Pasha [a local political authority] can take it from me. I
> have an estate; its taxes now amount to 5,000 piastres a year;
> he can raise them to 8,000 or 10,000. He may require it to
> furnish him with camels, oxen, or corn; he can take all the

1

able-bodied men in the village as recruits; he may take all its
inhabitants—men, women and children—and send them to
dig a canal in the desert. When he has rendered it incapable
of paying its taxes, he may seize it for arrears and grant it to
one of his favorites. No property, no rank, no institution is
safe except the few who enjoy European protection. . . . My
taxes may have been fully paid, but if my neighbors are in
arrears, the Nazar (the local tax-gatherer) comes to me. If I
plead poverty, he bastinadoes me [a method of punishment,
consisting of blows with a stick on the soles of the feet or
buttocks] to ascertain the truth of the plea. If he can get
nothing out of me by fear or by blows he seizes my land. . . .
What is called government in Egypt . . . is one vast system of
robbery.[2]

The lessons that the classical economists drew from such situations were very clear. An example can be taken from William
Huskisson's *Essays on Political Economy*, published in 1830:

The establishment of the right to property is essential to the
progress of civilization, and where no such right is acknowledged and maintained, barbarism and indigence will prevail.
In several of the countries of the East, where despotic monarchs rule, the reward of his toil is not secured to the labourer,
and the lives and properties of all classes of society are at the
sole disposal of a tyrant. It seems to be impossible, under such
circumstances, that there can exist adequate motives for
industrious exertion, beyond what is necessary to obtain the
means of ordinary subsistence. No one will toil and patiently
endure for the purpose of acquiring property, of the enjoyment of which he is far from being assured. . . . Security of
persons and to property is the ultimate object and end of the
institution of government. Unless this is kept constantly in
view, the motive for conceding authority to public officers is
misunderstood. . . . The people will take sufficient care of
their own happiness, if they enjoy full security themselves,
and remain free from all constraints that are not absolutely
necessary for the security of the persons and property of other

parties. . . . The maintenance of full security [of private property] is the only good reason, which can ultimately be assigned for keeping up civil and military establishments.[3]

For the classical economists, therefore, the role of government—its only essential rationale for existence—was the legal protection of individual rights to life and property. This was the essence, in their view, of the meaning of "good government."[4] What was expected from the law was the impartial enforcement of justice among the members of the society. And a hallmark of such justice was respect for freedom of contract (or association). Individuals were assumed to know their own interests far better than any legislator or bureaucrat. They were assumed to be better judges of the potential advantages from opportunities for trade and exchange than any appointed regulator who might be assigned to dictate the terms under which men would be allowed to transact. For government to contribute its part to the establishment and preservation of justice, it was expected to not interfere with the voluntary relationships among men, unless there occurred the private use of force or fraud, or if such arrangements infringed on the rights of third parties not part of the contractual relationship.[5]

When the classical economists of the eighteenth and nineteenth centuries made their case for protection of life and property by pointing to extreme cases in which individuals in some parts of the world seemed to possess almost no rights, they were using these examples as a background for criticisms of their own societies in which the state abridged and regulated the use of private property. Under the system of mercantilism, few corners of the marketplace were free from the control of the state. And in the name of improving the economic well-being of the nation as a whole, the kings of seventeenth- and eighteenth-century Europe bestowed various privileges, favors, and monopolies on selected manufacturers, merchants, and agricultural interests.

Beginning with the French Physiocrats and the Scottish moral philosophers (among whom were David Hume and Adam Smith), the classical economists demonstrated that such systems of privilege, favor, and monopoly were restraints on improvements of the "wealth of nations." What was needed was the freeing of production, trade, and commerce from the heavy hand of government control. In place of the mercantilists' regulated economy, the classical economists advocated what Adam Smith called a "system of natural liberty." Government should be limited to the protection of people's life, liberty, and property from domestic and foreign aggression, and the provision of a small handful of "public works." Said Smith:

> All systems of either preference or restraint, therefore, being thus completely taken away, the obvious and simple system of natural liberty establishes itself of its own accord. Every man, as long as he does not violate the laws of justice, is left perfectly free to pursue his own interest his own way, and to bring both his industry and capital into competition with those of any other man, or order of men. The sovereign is completely discharged from a duty, in the attempting to perform which he must be exposed to innumerable delusions, and for the proper performance of which no human wisdom or knowledge could ever be sufficient; the duty of superintending the industry of private people, and of directing it towards employments most suitable to the interest of the society.[6]

For the first hundred and fifty years, Americans lived under an economic system that came closer to Smith's ideal of natural liberty than any other in the history of the world. The United States grew into an industrial giant that absorbed tens of millions of immigrants from around the globe and produced the highest standard of living ever known in human history. But most of all what it gave Americans was freedom: freedom for individuals to live their own lives, peacefully pursuing their own ends in voluntary association and exchange with their fellow men for mutual benefit. But especially during the last sixty years government in America has increasingly narrowed the arena of freedom. Government oversees, regulates, controls, supervises, and directs to one degree or another everything that we do in our daily lives. The law no longer serves to protect our rights as individuals, but to abridge them. The law, as the great French economist Frederic Bastiat expressed it, is "perverted."[7] It no longer impartially secures and protects our individual rights to life, liberty, and property; instead government uses the law to once again bestow privileges, favors, and political benefits on some groups in the society at the expense of others.

Just as a society without law and a government sufficiently strong to enforce it would be reduced to a state of mutual plunder and violence, a government that uses its police power to violate people's rights also produces a condition of plunder and violence. "Austrian School" economist Ludwig von Mises, in whose name these annual lectures at Hillsdale College are dedicated, emphasized the point in very clear terms:

> With human nature as it is, the state is a necessary and indispensable institution. The state is, if properly administered, the foundation of society, of human cooperation and civilization. It is the most beneficial and most useful instrument in the endeavors of man to promote human happiness and welfare. But it is a tool and a means only, not the ultimate goal. It is not God. It is simply compulsion and coercion; it is the police power. . . . He who says: "The state is God," deifies arms and prisons. The worship of the state is the worship of force. There is no more dangerous menace to civilization than a government of incompetent, corrupt and vile men. The worst evils which mankind ever had to endure were inflicted by bad governments. The state can be and has often been in the course of history the main source of mischief and disaster.[8]

Mises also explained the purpose of law and the rule of law:

> State and government are nothing else than the social apparatus of violent coercion and repression. Such an apparatus, the police power, is indispensable in order to prevent antisocial individuals and bands from destroying social cooperation. . . . But violence and oppression are nonetheless evils and corrupt those in charge of their application. It is necessary to restrict the power of those in office lest they become absolute despots. . . . It is the social function of the laws to curb the arbitrariness of the police. The rule of law

restricts the arbitrariness of the officers as much as possible. It strictly limits their discretion and thus assigns to the citizens a sphere in which they are free to act without being frustrated by government interference. . . . Liberty can be realized only within an established state ready to prevent a gangster from killing and robbing his weaker fellows. But it is the rule of law alone which hinders the rulers from turning themselves into the worst gangsters. . . . The rule of law, or limited government, as safeguarded by constitutions and bills of rights, is the characteristic mark of [Western] civilization. It was the rule of law that brought about the marvelous achievements of modern capitalism.[9]

In comparison to a hundred years or even in comparison to fifty years ago, today's United States government is unrestrained. Our income is taxed away for redistribution programs; our property is seized under arbitrary and unrestricted asset forfeiture laws; our enterprises and businesses are regulated and licensed; our children are controlled and manipulated in government schools; the use of privately owned land is under environmental rules that strip us of any real control over what on paper is supposed to be ours; our personal associations and work place relationships are monitored and revised by the state for purposes of "political correctness." What we watch on television, eat at the dinner table, or consume for enjoyment and relaxation are supervised, rated, and restricted by the government. Our only consolation is the thought that many other parts of the world are even less free than our own. And, thus, in comparison we still remain one of the freest countries on earth. But this is all in relative comparison. In absolute terms we are no longer the free people the Founding Fathers intended under the Constitution, the Bill of Rights, and the rule of law.

The 1997 Ludwig von Mises Lectures, "Between Power and Liberty: Economics and the Law," published here as Volume 25 in the Champions of Freedom series, were devoted to the loss of our economic freedom to the state. The speakers explained the freedoms we have lost, the methods through which the government now controls our lives in the marketplace, and how we might reverse this trend and return to the path of liberty.

Free market economists like Mises have always understood that human freedom stands or falls with the protection and respect for private property—not merely private ownership in name only, but in reality. Either "We the People" determine how our private property will be applied and used guided by the market opportunities we individually find for mutual gains from trade, or the government controls, guides, and dictates the use of that property.

Seventy years ago, Mises reminded us of the ultimate importance in the protection and sanctity of private property:

> Private property creates for the individual a sphere in which he is free of the state. It sets limits to the operation of the authoritarian will. It allows other forces to arise side by side with and in opposition to political power. It thus becomes the basis of all those activities that are free from violent interference on the part of the state. It is the soil in which the seeds of freedom are nurtured and in which the autonomy of the individual and ultimately all intellectual and material progress are rooted. . . . Whoever champions [private property] champions by the same token the preservation of the social bond that unites mankind, the preservation of culture and civilization.[10]

It is with the hope of preserving the free individual, the free society, and the system of private property and free enterprise upon which it is based, that the 1997 Ludwig von Mises Lectures are offered here in published form to the general reading public.

RICHARD M. EBELING
Ludwig von Mises Professor
of Economics
Hillsdale College

Notes

[1]Jean-Baptiste Say, *A Treatise on Political Economy* [1826] (New York: Augustus M. Kelley, Publishers, [1888] 1971), 127.
[2]Nassau W. Senior, *Industrial Efficiency and Social Economy*, Vol. 1 (New York: Henry Holt and Co., 1928), 81–82.

[3]William Huskisson, *Essays on Political Economy* [1830] (Canberra: Australian National University, 1976), 45–46, 62–63. William Huskisson was a member of the British Parliament, (1796–1801 and 1804–1830) and Secretary of State for War and the Colonies (1827–1828). See also Thomas Malthus, *An Essay on the Principle of Population, or a View of Its Past and Present Effects on Human Happiness,* 7th ed. [1872] (Fairfield, NJ: Augustus M. Kelley, Publishers, 1986), 88–92.

[4]See Samuel Read, *Political Economy, An Inquiry into the Natural Grounds of Right to Vendible Property or Wealth* [1829] (Fairfield, NJ: Augustus M. Kelley, Publishers, 1976), 154–76; also G. Poulett Scrope, *Principles of Political Economy, Deduced from the Natural Laws of Social Welfare* [1833] (New York: Augustus M. Kelley, Publishers, 1969), 21–27.

[5]See Albert Venn Dicey, *Lectures on the Relation Between Law and Public Opinion in England During the Nineteenth Century* [1905] (New Brunswick, NJ: Transaction Books, 1981), 146–58.

[6]Adam Smith, *The Wealth of Nations* [1776] (New York: The Modern Library, 1937), Book IV Ch. IX, 651.

[7]Frederic Bastiat, "The Law," *Selected Essays in Political Economy* (Princeton, NJ: D. Van Nostrand, Inc., 1964), 51–96.

[8]Ludwig von Mises, *Omnipotent Government: The Rise of the Total State and Total War* [1944] (New Rochelle, NY: Arlington House, 1969), 47.

[9]Ludwig von Mises, *Planned Chaos* (Irvington-on-Hudson, NY: Foundation for Economic Education, 1947), 63–66, reprinted in Mises, *Socialism: An Economic and Sociological Analysis* [1951, rev. ed.] (Indianapolis: Liberty Classics, 1981), 519–21.

[10]Ludwig von Mises, *Liberalism in the Classical Tradition* [1927] (Irvington-on-Hudson, NY: Foundation for Economic Education, 1978), 67–68, 87.

RICHARD M. EBELING

The Free Market and the Interventionist State

In 1926, Austrian economist Ludwig von Mises visited the United States on a lecture tour. Upon his return to Austria, he delivered a talk on "Changes in American Economic Policy" at a meeting of the Vienna Industrial Club. He explained:

> The United States has become great and rich under the power of an economic system that has set no limits on the free pursuit of the individual, and has thereby made room for the development of the country's productive power. America's unprecedented economic prosperity is not the result of the richness of the American land, but rather of the economic policy that understood how best to take advantage of the opportunities that the land offers. American economic policy has always rejected—and still rejects today—any protection for inferiority and uncompetitiveness over efficiency and competitiveness. The success of this policy has been so great that one would believe the Americans would never change it.[1]

But Mises went on to tell his Viennese audience that new voices were being heard in America, voices that claimed that America's economic system was not "rational" enough, that it was not democratic enough, because the voters did not have it in their immediate power to influence the direction of industrial development. Governmental controls were being introduced, not to nationalize private enterprise, but to direct it though various regulatory methods. In comparison to Europe, America was certainly noticeably less regulated. But there were strong trends moving the nation along the same heavily interventionist path Europe had been traveling for a long time. In the America of 1926, Mises observed, "Both political parties, the Republicans as well as the Democrats, are ready to take radical steps in this direction, in order to retain the votes of the electorate." He concluded that "the results from such a policy will be no different in America than from those 'achieved' in Europe."[2]

In Europe, the trend toward collectivism in the 1930s and 1940s took extreme forms. Socialism, communism, fascism, and Nazism were all tried on the other side of the Atlantic. They represented total rejection of a free economy and individual liberty. In America, the collectivist trend never went to such extremes, though Franklin D. Roosevelt's first New Deal came very close to the fascist model.[3]

The Free Market Economy and Interventionism

Socialism, communism, fascism, and Nazism are now all but dead. They failed miserably. But they have been replaced by what is merely another more watered-down form of collectivism that may be called "interventionism." Indeed, interventionism is the predominant economic system in the world today. In 1929, Mises published a collection of essays under the title *Critique of Interventionism.* He argued,

> Nearly all writers on economic policy and nearly all statesmen and party leaders are seeking an ideal system which, in their belief, is neither [purely] capitalistic nor socialistic, is based neither on [unrestricted] private property in the means of production nor on public property. They are searching for a system of private property that is hampered, regulated, and directed through government intervention and other social forces, such as labor unions. We call such an economic policy *interventionism*, the system itself the *hampered market order*.[4]

He added, "All its followers and advocates fully agree that it is the correct policy for the coming decades, yea, even the coming generations. And all agree that interventionism constitutes an economic policy that will prevail in the foreseeable future."[5]

Definitions

With the demise of communism, public policy—especially in the Western world—is back to where it was when Mises wrote these words nearly seventy years ago. Comprehensive government ownership of the means of production and a fully centralized planned economy have very few adherents left, even "on the left." At the same time, in spite of all the casual rhetoric about the triumph of capitalism, what is defined as a "free market economy" contains a great deal of government intervention. The following eight points, I suggest, define the genuine free market economy:

1. All means of production are privately owned.
2. The use of the means of production is under the control of private owners who may be individuals or corporate entities.
3. Consumer demands determine how the means of production will be used.
4. Competitive forces of supply and demand determine the prices for consumer goods and the various factors of production such as labor.
5. The success or failure of individual and corporate enterprises is determined by the profits or losses these enterprises earn, based on their greater or lesser ability to satisfy consumer demand in competition with their rivals in the marketplace.
6. The market is not confined to domestic transactions and includes freedom of international trade.
7. The monetary system is based on a market-determined commodity (e.g., gold or silver), and the banking system is private and competitive, neither controlled nor regulated by government.
8. Government is limited in its activities to the enforcement and protection of life, liberty, and property.

When government merely serves as a protector of life, liberty, and property, it does not "intervene" in the economy. It respects and protects rights of ownership. It ensures that the transfer of property only occurs through a gift or through a mutually agreed-upon exchange. It ensures that as long as individuals do not infringe upon or violate the equal rights of others (through acts of violence or fraud), they are not molested, harmed, or dispossessed of their own property.[6]

While they may be open to some refinement, the eight points outlined above comprise what Mises referred to as the "unhampered economy." Unfortunately, many modern politicians and academics who say they endorse such a free market economy are willing to tolerate a great deal of intervention. One notable example is Robert Skidelsky, a professor of political economy at Warwick University in England. Professor Skidelsky is the widely respected author of a multi-volume biography of John Maynard Keynes.[7] He has also written that former communist countries must move toward the establishment of market institutions if they are to stabilize their economies and raise standards of living.[8] In his most recent book, *The Road from Serfdom,* he insightfully analyzes how socialist and welfare-statist ideas came to dominate economic theory and government policy in the twentieth century.[9] Many of his eloquent and powerful criticisms of these forms of collectivism are based on the writings of Friedrich A. Hayek, the famous Austrian School economist and Nobel laureate. And Professor Skidelsky declares that he is an advocate of the free market.

But when it comes to identifying the role of government in his conception of the market order, he assumes that government must be responsible for a social safety net that includes Social Security and unemployment compensation; must have discretionary monetary and fiscal powers to support desired levels of employment and output; must regulate industry to assure "competitive" conditions in the market and "fair" labor conditions for workers; and must directly supply certain goods and services which the market allegedly does not provide. I do not mean to single out Skidelsky for any special criticism. He is a very careful and thoughtful scholar. His is just one recent and clear statement of this point of view. Indeed, many others who are "on the right" believe that government should institute some or all of these "public policies."

It is important to appreciate, however, that the very notion of "public policy," as the term is almost always used, implies government intervention in the market in ways that are simply inconsistent with a genuine free market economy. Interventionism as public policy is not consistent with the free market since its very purpose, by intention, is to prevent or modify the outcomes of the market.[10] Here are the eight points of interventionism:

1. The private ownership of the means of production is restricted or abridged.
2. The use of the means of production by private owners is prohibited, limited, or regulated.
3. The users of the means of production are prevented from being guided solely by consumer demand.
4. Government influences or controls the formation of prices for consumer goods and/or the factors of production.
5. Government reduces the impact of market supply and demand on the success or failure of various enterprises while increasing its own influence and control over market incomes through such artificial means as pricing and production regulations, limits on freedom of entry into segments of the market, and direct or indirect subsidies.
6. Free entry into the domestic market by potential foreign rivals is discouraged or outlawed through import prohibitions, quotas, or tariffs.
7. The monetary system is regulated by government for the purpose of influencing what is used as money, the value of money, and the rate at which the quantity of money is increased or decreased. And all these are used as tools for affecting employment, output, and growth in the economy.
8. Government's role is not limited to the protection of life, liberty, and property.

It is important to note that the "public policies" these eight points represent must be implemented through violent means. Only the threat or use of force can make people follow courses of action that differ from the ones that they would have peacefully taken if it were not for government intervention.[11] There is really nothing "public" about these policies after all; they are coercive policies.

Contrast these policies with the policies of a free market, or unhampered economy, as we have defined it. What is most striking is the voluntary nature of economic arrangements. The means of production are privately owned and the owners are free to determine how those means will be employed. Thus, control over the means of production is depoliticized. Since this control is not located in one place but is dispersed among a wide segment of the society's population, it is also decentralized. Individuals control the means through which they can maintain and improve their own circumstances and they are not dependent upon a single political source for employment or the necessities and luxuries of life.[12] But it is not just the owners of the means of production who have a high degree of autonomy in the free market economy; consumers do, too, since they are the ones who determine what products and services will be in demand.

The Law of Association

The basis of society, Mises always emphasized, is what he called "the law of association." Men can more successfully improve their individual condition through cooperation, and the means through which that cooperation can be made most productive is the division of labor. By taking advantage of individual talents and circumstances through specialization, the total quantity and quality of society's output can be dramatically improved. Individuals do not have to try to satisfy all their own wants through isolated activity.[13] And once they specialize their activities, they become interdependent; they rely upon each other for the vast majority of goods and services they desire. But it is this very interdependency that gives production its real and true social character. If men are to acquire from others what they desire, they must devote their energies to producing what others are willing to accept in trade. The fundamental rule of the market is mutual agreement and voluntary exchange. Each member of society must orient his activities toward serving the wants of at least some of the other members in an unending circle of trade. The Scottish moral philosopher Adam Smith observed over two hundred years ago:

[M]an has almost constant occasion for the help of his brethren, and it is in vain for him to expect it from their benevolence only. He will be more likely to prevail if he can interest their self-love in his favour, and shew them that it is to their own advantage to do for him what he requires of them. Whosoever offers to another a bargain of any kind, proposes to do this. Give me that which I want, and you shall have this which you want, is the meaning of every such offer; and it is in this manner that we obtain from one another the far greater part of those good offices which we stand in need of. It is not from the benevolence of the butcher, the brewer, or the baker, that we expect our dinner, but from their regard for their own interest. We address ourselves, not to their humanity, but to their self-love, and never talk to them of our own necessities but of their own advantages.[14]

This is what assures that consumer demand guides the uses for which the means of production are applied. Each individual must find a way to satisfy some of the needs of others before he can satisfy his own wants and desires. As a result, the prices for consumer goods and the factors of production are not decreed by government but are formed in the marketplace through the competitive forces of supply and demand. Success or failure is determined by the profits and losses earned on the basis of the greater or lesser ability to meet consumer demand in competition with rivals in the marketplace.[15] In a real sense, therefore, capitalism is the only true "public policy." Every person's private interest in the marketplace is socially oriented. Through the incentives of profit and loss, each owner of means of production must direct the use of the resources under his control into those channels which he believes will most likely best serve his fellow men. In the social system of division of labor, it is not necessary for each consumer to control directly the resources upon which his wants and desires depend. The market "socializes" their use on the behalf of consumers by making each actual owner of the means of production dependent upon successful sales to earn his own livelihood.[16]

The Political Economy of Interventionism:
Rationales and Replies

Just as interventionism modifies people's behavior through coercion, it also modifies market outcomes. Why do its advocates believe this is necessary and/or desirable? It is possible to classify their rationales under three general headings: economic theory, social justice, and public interest.

Economic Theory

Neoclassical, or mainstream, economics has constructed a theory of market competition that has continued to serve as the conceptual benchmark for judging and evaluating actual market situations. "Perfect competition" is defined as a situation in which the following conditions are assumed to exist:[17]

1. There are so many buyers and sellers on both sides of the market that no one buyer or seller believes that he can influence the price in the market in which he buys or sells. Each buyer and seller takes the market price as "given." And each adjusts the amount he buys or sells at that given price to maximize the utility (personal satisfaction) or profit received from his purchases or sales.

2. Each seller markets a product that is exactly like those sold by all the other sellers in the same market. So the buyer does not care from whom he buys because each seller offers a good that can be substituted for the ones offered by his rivals.

3. There are no technological or other impediments that prevent resources from being rapidly reallocated from one industry or sector of the market to another in the face of even the smallest changes in supply and demand conditions anywhere in the economy. The instant that a profit opportunity or a loss situation arises anywhere in the market, resources are reallocated to assure that they are exactly where they should be to assure "optimal" output everywhere in the market.

4. All participants in the market possess perfect (or sufficient) knowledge to assure that no buyer ever pays a higher price and no seller ever accepts a lower price than the "objective" or "real" market condition dictates that they should. This means that profits are not earned and losses are not suffered by the participants in the market, since buyers and sellers would not pass up profits that could be earned or suffer losses that could be avoided.

These four conditions are usually considered to constitute the standard for judging a market as being "efficient" or "optimal" in terms of pricing and production. It is true that during the last several decades neoclassical economists have undertaken "immanent criticisms" of the framework, pointing out that there may be rational reasons why the conception of a "perfect market" may not always be accurate. For example, there may be "transaction costs" involved in consummating exchanges among market participants that produce market outcomes that are different from the pattern that would exist if such "costs" were zero.[18] Or the market situation may be less than optimal because the costs of acquiring information at the margin may exceed the anticipated benefit from acquiring additional knowledge about possible opportunities.[19] Adding these subsidiary qualifications leads some neoclassical economists to take a "Panglossian" view; they believe that there can be no better world than the one we are living in since whatever the world produces in terms of market supplies and demands is the best that can be hoped for, given these costs of doing business and acquiring information. And this reasoning can also be turned around so the case can be made that any existing degree of government intervention is also optimal.

Hayek argued against the entire conception of perfect competition fifty years ago in his essay, "The Meaning of Competition."[20] As defined in textbooks over the decades, perfect competition explains a state of affairs in which it is assumed that the *process* of competition has already brought about a state of fully balanced equilibrium, without any explanation of how such a state of equilibrium would have come about.[21] Another way of saying this is that in neoclassical economics the term "competition" is used as a *noun* rather than as a *verb*. That is to say, it is invariably portrayed as a static state or situation rather than as a series of actions or activities. In colloquial conversation, "to compete" is thought of as a circumstance under which the participants act in a manner to "do better" than their rivals. To "do better" in the marketplace means to offer a lower price or a different product or an improved and more attractive commodity or service. By necessity, to compete in this sense means to change the *price* in a way that customers find it more profitable to buy from one particular seller rather than the next fellow. It means to *differentiate the product* from the products of rivals by offering qualities or characteristics that are more attractive. It means to *discover* or *create* profit opportunities, either by being alert to price discrepancies between the potential selling price and the cost prices that others have not noticed or by inventing less costly ways of making a product.

Ironically, according to standard textbook conceptions of competition, these types of actions are often considered the hallmarks of *anticompetitive* behavior.[22] Interventions have sometimes been advocated in the past to prevent market competitors from competing in the name of establishing a situation resembling a condition of "perfect competition."[23] From the perspective of Austrian School economists like Mises and Hayek, such interventions are completely misplaced.[24] Once we drop the assumption of "perfect" or "sufficient" knowledge, the entire neoclassical view of competition is shown to be misdirected. Instead, competition, as Hayek has referred to it, can be regarded as a "discovery procedure."[25] In the actual market based on a system of division of labor, individuals inevitably come to possess not only specialized skills and productive abilities—as Adam Smith and many early classical economists forcefully argued—but also specialized knowledge as well.[26] The specialization of knowledge that naturally accompanies a division of labor means that the market participants must find some way to integrate their respective activities with each other for a mutual coordination of their plans.

Prices serve this role in the market. They do so as cost estimators and information disseminators. If resources are to be efficiently applied among their alternative uses in the market, decisionmakers must have some way of finding out their relative market worth in different productive uses. The resource prices that arise through the competitive process of market bids for their ownership or use are composite summaries of entrepreneurial judgments concerning their value in competing lines of production. Each employer of factors of production must weigh what resources are believed to be worth to him, given his expectations of the prices consumers might be willing to pay for finished goods after a production process is completed and a commodity or service is ready for sale. The rivalrous bids of employers on the one side and the search for the most remunerative employment by owners of the factors of production on the other side generate the prices for resources and labor.

The resulting prices that emerge from consummated transactions serve as the tools for "economic calculation" used by decisionmakers concerning which combinations of resources will minimize their costs of production. Market-based pricing and resource use assure that resources are always tending to be applied to their most highly valued uses, and never *permanently* kept in some productive application that represents a lower-valued use than some other for which they could be utilized.[27] But prices are not "static" phenomena. Since they are reflections of "subjective" valuations and appraisals of consumers, entrepreneurs, and resource owners, anything that changes those subjective valuations and appraisals will bring about changes in market prices. And every change in prices originating in one corner of the market will then generate changes in consumer and producer plans in other corners of the market. Hayek emphasized that it is only through this process of changed price bids and offers for goods and resources that individuals can effectively inform others about new supply and demand conditions. Then the others respond by "recalculating" the most efficient ways to undertake their consumption and production plans, given the new configuration of prices with which they are confronted in the market.

The competitive discovery procedure that Hayek described does not just concern consumption decisions and production plans, given changes in the prices of the marketplace. It also concerns the profit incentives and rivalry in the market, out of which market participants and decisionmakers are driven to unearth new opportunities and create new possibilities. Which of these new opportunities and possibilities will pay off? Which goods and services will consumers buy? What prices and qualities will be better than some rival could offer? These questions can only be answered through the market's competitive process.[28]

The same logic applies to any endeavor that involves competition. Look at the world of sports, for example. Regardless of the facts known about the players and the win–loss records of the teams, the outcome of a game cannot be known in advance. Too many variables are involved. Each has unique and nondeterministic properties. The "games of the market," to use Hayek's metaphor, are equally nondeterministic.[29] Competitors in the free market economy only discover their own potential by being alert to new opportunities, by imagining new ways of undertaking production, by creating new goods and services, and by responding to new incentives. How they can and will react to changing market situations—including their responses to competitors who constantly challenge them with rival innovations and creations—will only emerge in the process of finding themselves in ever-new circumstances. The responses will be the result of individuals thinking about new situations and possibilities. And no one knows their own future thoughts. If they did, those thoughts would then be today's and not tomorrow's.

What public policy should be concerned with is the clear delineation and enforcement of the rules. In the unhampered economy, this means legal recognition and enforcement of individual rights to life, liberty, and property. As long as the rules are followed and each participant renounces the use of force and fraud in his dealings with others, each is left free to pursue his own ends, apply the means of production under his ownership and disposal, and interact with his fellow free men as he finds most advantageous. Outcomes are unplanned, and spontaneous results emerge from the actions and interactions of all the participants in the market. The rules also ensure that each participant will tend to apply his knowledge, ability, and potential in ways that serve the interests of the other members of society. This allows for much greater freedom, flexibility, and creativity than if government intervenes in an attempt to "plan" the results by regulating the actions and the "play" of the market process.[30]

From this "Austrian" perspective, neither the market nor competition need be "perfect" as it is usually formulated in neoclassical economic theory. Markets and competition and efficiency are working as best as they can as long as:

1. Markets are not restricted or closed by political regulation.
2. Taxes do not act as barriers to savings and capital formation.
3. Interventionist policies do not attempt to deflect market processes from the course they naturally follow guided by the profit motive in the service of consumer demand.

Social Justice

"Welfare state" interventions are typically proposed in the name of "social justice." The assumptions behind the appeal for "social justice" are several. The first assumption is that an unhampered economy will tend to generate exploitation. Some members of the society will prey on others, and the state should therefore intervene to redress presumed imbalances in "power." The second assumption is that even if the unhampered economy does not directly exploit individuals, it does create inequalities in income and wealth that unfairly benefit some at the expense of others. Such unfairness requires compensation through income redistribution. Third, however efficient the free market may be, its competitive flexibility introduces degrees of insecurity that need to be compensated for by state interventions that either slow down the pace of change or supply employment and income guarantees to those adversely affected by market-induced changes. Regardless of the form of the argument, all the proposed policies involve direct or indirect redistribution of income through political transfers. Unless it involves brute confiscation (he who has the political power has the "right" to coerce the transfers he wants), every appeal to social justice must rest on some notion of "fairness" in income distribution or employment entitlement.

The charge that workers are exploited by employers goes back to the socialist critique of capitalist society that was first developed in the early nineteenth century and that reached its climax in the writings of Karl Marx. It would have validity only if it could be demonstrated that some are "forced" to work for others at terms of employment to which the "exploited" have not freely agreed. But in a free market economy a fundamental principle upon which the system operates is the rule of voluntary agreement. No individual may be coerced into buying from another, working for another, or selling to another at terms that are not freely agreed upon. By definition, a free market excludes exploitation.

The countercharge of modern liberals, socialists, and Marxists is that the free market economy is inherently exploitative because the means of production are owned and controlled by a small minority of the members of the society. Their nearly exclusive control over land, machinery, factories, and financial capital means that the workers must accept whatever terms the employers dictate because they have no real choice if they are to earn a living. They may appear to be free, but in reality, their fate is sealed. The trouble is that this is not an economic assumption; it is fatalism, pure and simple. It fails to see human beings as anything more than pawns, without brains, without resourcefulness, without dignity.

It is true that, in the division of labor, it naturally follows that only a minority of a society's members specialize in the provision of any particular good or service. But no minority can force workers to work or force buyers to buy. A minority may own the means of production, but the way in which those means are utilized is really up to the much larger consuming majorities. Barbers are a minority who enjoy a virtual "monopoly" because they have the required skills and own the means of production. But they are not exploiting the majority simply by offering haircuts.

In the market, it will always be a minority that owns the means of production and that serves as the entrepreneurial force guiding the use of those means in various lines of production. Interest, inclination, ability, persistence, and a taste for risk-taking are not qualities that all men share in equal measures. Only a few have the willingness and capacity to be "captains of industry." Successful entrepreneurship is more a gift than a result of training. The ability to "read" the market, to have a "feel" for where consumer demand is shifting, to have a "sense" of how to respond to competitors—these are not things that can be learned from textbooks or MBA programs. And while formal education and training may provide types of knowledge that can assist and enhance an entrepreneur's potential, they cannot guarantee success. At the same time, many individuals in the society are risk-averse or unsure of their ability. They prefer the contractual salary income that assures them a certain fixed sum every month. Others are unwilling to make the personal sacrifices that self-employment and entrepreneurship require. The individual who runs his own business or even manages a business for others rarely can afford to punch out at five o'clock. Still others are unwilling to forego present consumption to accumulate the savings that are essential for starting up or expanding a business. And some who are willing to try simply end up making too many mistakes and go out of business. These are all aspects and consequences of the natural inequality among individuals.

Finally, the charge of economic exploitation was refuted a little over a hundred years ago by the economist Eugen von Böhm-Bawerk.[31] In developing the Austrian School theory of capital and interest, Böhm-Bawerk pointed out that all processes of production involve time. If the period of production is of any significant length of time, then those who are undertaking the manufacture of a product must somehow be able to sustain themselves until the commodity being produced is ready for sale and earns a price greater than or at least equal to its costs from members of the buying public. If those employed in making this good are unwilling or unable to sustain themselves until the product is sold, then someone must advance them the wages that will enable them to buy the various goods and services they may need or desire. This, Böhm-Bawerk explained, is the role of the capitalist. By saving, the capitalist foregoes consumption or other uses for which he could have applied his own wealth in the present and over the period of production. His savings represent the source of the workers' wages during the production process. What Marx called the capitalists' "exploitative profits," Böhm-Bawerk showed to be, in fact, the implicit interest payment for performing an extremely valuable service: providing the needed savings to pay workers during time-consuming, "round-about" processes of production. As long as there is free competition in the market for factors of production and as long as individuals are politically unrestricted from starting their own business for purposes of self-employment, there can be no justification for a charge of "exploitation."

If the state intervenes in an attempt to redress what is claimed to be an imbalance of "power" in the bargaining process of the market, it can only do so by restricting the freedom of some to benefit others.[32] If, for example, it makes trade unionism and collective bargaining mandatory, it must restrict the freedom of employers and nonunion members who might otherwise have chosen to enter into mutually agreed upon terms of employment. The only way that such an abridgment of ability to contract freely can be enforced is if the state either uses its monopoly of physical force to prevent such agreements or (implicitly or explicitly) delegates such coercive power to collective bargaining trade unions.[33] Enhancing "labor's power" in this situation means to empower some workers with the coercive ability to impose upon others terms of trade more to their liking. If all workers who might be interested in finding or maintaining employment with a particular employer or group of employers agreed with advocates of collective bargaining, then political empowerment would not be needed. The employers would not be able to find any workers with the skills or experience desired who would be willing to accept the jobs that were available at the wages being offered. That coercion must be introduced demonstrates that there are some workers with the minimum skills and experience the employers view as necessary who would be willing to accept employment at a wage that underbids the minimum wage the advocates of collective bargaining are demanding.

This, of course, does not mean that the terms accepted in an exchange are always the ones workers may most prefer. Most individuals would prefer to pay one dollar instead of twenty dollars for an excellent steak dinner in an nice restaurant. The fact that many do go to restaurants and pay a higher price for a steak dinner demonstrates that, given personal preferences and the occasion, they value the dinner in that restaurant more than the price they pay for it. The same applies to acceptance of employment; given an individual's wishes to possess income to buy certain things in the market and given the employment opportunities prevailing in the market for his particular skills and experience, he will accept the most attractive job available.

As I indicated earlier, another rationale for social justice claims that the market generates unfair inequalities in income and wealth that require the state to rectify this "social injustice" through economic redistribution. But what is the standard for such social justice? Hayek has argued persuasively that in a market economy there is no way to judge whether the distribution of income is just or unjust. On the one hand, the relative income shares earned by individuals in a free market can be viewed as "just" in the sense that each individual receives what he has contracted for or earned as residual profits through the voluntary transactions of the marketplace. He has not received a contractual income or profit through either force or fraud. On the other hand, Hayek points out that free market incomes are earned not on the basis of merit, but rather on the basis of the value of services rendered.[34] The fact that an individual may have worked hard and to the best of his ability does not mean that the market will reward him with an income reflecting some measurement of his industriousness. He receives the income that reflects what his employer or consumers think his product or service is worth to them. If a rival were able to make a better or cheaper product with less effort and industriousness, that rival would be likely to generate more sales and receive a higher income.[35]

Furthermore, in the free market economy, the relative income shares earned by individuals are not determined according to any economywide plan or design. They are the outcomes of market transactions that have no economywide goal or purpose. The distribution of income is actually one of the "unintended consequences" of the overall market process. No plan or prior arrangement dictates or determines how much each will earn as a result of transactions in the marketplace. Nor is income distributed among the members of the society after the production and sales processes have been completed. Earned incomes arise out of competitive buying, selling, and contracting and are the results of an ongoing market process.

To redistribute income according to "social justice" requires a standard to determine what each member of the society "deserves." But Hayek demonstrates conclusively that no such standard exists. To merely refer to "industriousness," "goodness," and "need" is not sufficient. How can any one of these be objectively defined and measured? How is the distributional share to be determined if an individual has "many needs," is "fairly industrious," but is only moderately "good"? How does this compare with a person who has "a few simple needs," "oozes with goodness," but is only "slightly industrious"? Does it matter if he has a small or large family, or "bright" or "dumb" children? With good cause, Hayek likened the pursuit of "social justice" to chasing after a mirage. A mirage seems real when it lies off in the distance, but it vanishes into nothing as you approach it.

The third rationale for social justice is the assumption that the very flexibility and efficiency of the free economy are actually great drawbacks because they cause changes and insecurities in income and employment. The state needs to compensate by "adjusting" income and making employment "secure." While this is a hot topic today, a summary of this rationale was given by Allen G. B. Fisher fifty years ago, during the post-World War II period of dramatic change and readjustment to peacetime conditions:

> The problem of personal security is essentially only one aspect of the wider problem of the general stability of the economy within which the individual has to earn his living. To this wider problem there are, in general, two contrasted methods of approach. One is to examine our economy sector by sector, and probably giving priority to those which have recently suffered most from instability, and then to endeavor by piecemeal action to stabilize in turn each sector of the economy, in the hope that eventually stability for the economy as a whole may emerge as a by-product from these successive but partial stabilizing processes. From the standpoint of the individual, this means that we attempt to ensure his security by establishing or restoring him to the place in the economy to which he believes himself to have a customary right. On the other hand, we may prefer to examine the economy as a whole, more or less in the analogy of a growing, living

organism, the healthy growth of which is closely dependent upon a similar condition in each part of it, and therefore set ourselves the task of fostering conditions favorable to the healthy development of the whole, in the belief that the adjustment of its several parts to the constantly recurring changes in basic conditions offers the best hopes for a reasonable degree of security in each one of them. Stability for the economy as a whole is then regarded as quite consistent with frequent and continuous changes in the places occupied in it by different individuals, and will indeed often be unattainable unless such changes are made.[36]

The importance of continuous adjustment to market change was also summarized by Fisher in an earlier essay:

The problem of production in a progressive society is the problem, then, of providing in the correct order and the proper proportions the goods and services which people with rising real incomes are likely to wish to purchase. . . . For, quite apart from changes in taste or fashion, rising standards of living will inevitably cause changes in the proportions which at some earlier date seemed to be appropriate, and so long as standards of living continue to rise, there will be continuous changes in the appropriate proportions, so that the economic problem of production will be constantly requiring new solutions. Changes in the proportions between different kinds of production, in their relative importance as fields for employment and investment, are, however, impossible unless there are constant transfers of resources, of labor and of capital, from the old and well-established industries to new and more risky industries. These changes often cause inconvenience to the individuals who have to make them, the labourers who have to change their occupation, and the capitalists who have to risk the loss of capital, and in consequence the changes are resisted. But unless the changes are made, not only is there no material progress, but the whole organization of production is dislocated and jammed, and we are threatened with definite retrogression.[37]

Any change in any part of the market economy necessarily results in the need for various types of adjustments in other parts of the market. Such adjustments always carry the potential for profit or loss. A system founded on the premise of voluntary exchange is one in which each participant must accept the fact that his success or failure is dependent upon whether he has succeeded in producing and offering for sale a product that others in the society value and whether they will pay more for that product than it cost to produce. If he has misjudged what the consumers want and the price they are willing to pay for what he brings to market, he suffers a loss rather than a profit. But that loss can have an important, positive impact on his business. A loss is "feedback"— direct information from the marketplace. It tells him that he has channeled his efforts in the wrong direction. It reveals that consumers prefer some other commodity, or that his rivals can make a similar product at a lower cost or with more attractive qualities. A successful entrepreneur learns from this feedback and makes appropriate changes.[38] He is like the helmsman who uses a compass to keep his ship on the right course. Imagine what a disaster it would be if some other force (like government) were to "adjust" his compass through intervention. He would surely end up shipwrecked or adrift.

Every innovation and improvement in the quality and available quantity of goods brought to market involves disruptions of the status quo that need adjustment, but not the kind of blind adjustment government offers. New technologies and new products replace old ones. New patterns increase consumer demand for some goods and decrease it for others. The employers' demand for certain types of labor increases for the goods in higher demand, and decreases for those in lower demand. If an economy is to adapt easily and rapidly to changing circumstances, every individual experiencing change in his respective corner of the market must be willing to respond appropriately. He must accept what the market dictates. But this "dictation" of the market does not involve the threat or use of force. Rather, it is merely a changing set of monetary rewards that the market offers for the performance of different activities. Each individual is free to respond as he considers best. As Edwin Cannan once expressed it, "Modern civilization, nearly all civilization, is based on the principle of making things pleasant for those who please the market and unpleasant for those who fail to do so." [39] If it is not the reward and punishment of profit and loss that guide people in their actions, then it will have to be some form of coercion. [40]

There are dangers when people turn to state intervention for protection and security from the winds of peaceful market change. The first is that the only way that the state can provide subsidies to support loss-making producers is through taxing those who are successful and profit-making. This weakens the incentive of the successful to be as industrious and alert to market opportunities as before. It also redistributes resources away from the production of goods that consumers actually want and for which they are willing to pay. The second danger is that once the state becomes a mechanism through which political protections and privileges may be received, individuals will have incentives to devote their time and wealth to the acquisition of favors from the state instead of using them to manufacture products that consumers want to buy. The third danger is that those who are meant to be the recipients of assistance from the state often end up being harmed rather than helped. Saving them from their own failures and mistakes ensures that they will not learn how to adapt. Such assistance creates a politics and psychology of dependency that traps many of the poor in the status of a permanent underclass that government support was supposed to eliminate. [41]

The need for such adjustment in the face of change is often more difficult for those who are employees, and not employers, to appreciate fully. In a system based on the division of labor, those who work for a contractual salary usually never come into direct contact with the consumers, the ultimate purchasers of the commodity which their labor has helped produce. The required adjustments the employer concludes he must introduce into the enterprise (on the basis of his reading of the existing and expected market conditions) often appear to the employee to be arbitrary. But they are not. It is the actual or expected buying patterns of the consumers that are imposing the necessity for change. [42] The failure to understand and appreciate this fact leads not only to resentment and unrest in the work force, but also can cause dislocations and distortions that delay adjustments to changing market conditions and increase the very economic instability intervention is meant to prevent.

Public Interest

The third rationale for interventionism is the "public interest." An individual or a group of individuals desire that the state intervene to achieve some end that they believe cannot be achieved voluntarily in the marketplace. There are many types of public interest pleading, but three of the most popular are based on national interest, environmental preservation, and public goods.

The "national interest" is perhaps the most commonly used type. The difficulty is that this term is as slippery as the "general welfare" and the "common good." It is a concept that can mean any number of things. That is why interventionists like it so much. They find it very useful in their attempts to restrict the freedoms of others for the attainment of goals they cannot achieve without compulsion. In a free market economy, however, the national interest (if this term is to have any meaning at all) is best served when government is confined to performing its limited functions of protecting life, liberty, and property. When each individual's liberty is secure, then the nation is secure. For the nation as a whole to have "interests" requiring government intervention, it would be necessary to agree upon a hierarchy of ends and means. This just is not possible, since the essence of a complex social order is the existence of diversity and divergence of chosen ends and selected means.

One of the core virtues of a free market economy based on a principle of voluntary exchange is that each member of the society sets his own goals; he pursues them by acquiring the means to his ends through voluntary exchange. Another way of saying this is that in the free market economy each individual is an end in himself and a means to the ends of others. As a consumer, he sets his own goals and others serve as the means to his ends in their role as producers. And, in turn, as a producer himself, he serves as the means to their ends. In this process, there is no need for any common or general agreement among the members of the society about literally thousands of complex issues. Sometimes, of course, men do share common goals and agree about their relative importance and the best means to achieve them. Then they form associations, clubs, and organizations. At the same time, those who do not share those goals, or who regard their relative importance differently, are not required to participate. They can go their own way, while respecting the right of those who choose various forms of collaboration.

"Environmental protection" is a second type of public interest pleading that rests on the false assumption that the free market economy is destroying our planet and that environmental controls must be imposed by the government. But one of the most vital functions performed by a free market economy is to assist in economizing on and preserving resources that people value and that are limited in supply. Nothing is a stronger force for conservation than the profit motive and the institution of private property. When a person is allowed to own something, he has an incentive to think twice before he wastes or abuses it. If he does waste or abuse what he owns, he directly suffers the cost because he loses the benefits that could have been his if only he had shown more care. And nothing is likely to result in greater abuse and misuse of something than when it is owned by nobody.

What is worth preserving in nature? What are the best means and methods to care for resources? Should we merely maintain what we have, or should we expand its supply? Have we set aside too much and, in fact, encroached too heavily on the attainment of other ends we also value? Even the most ardent environmentalist—unless he is one of those few extremists who would like to see man extinct in the belief that everything is worth preserving except the human race—believes that some land also must be used for residential housing, places of work, and non-wildlife recreation. To live, man must grow food, raise animals, and use resources for clothing, the daily amenities of life, and arts and sciences. The advantage of leaving these problems to the marketplace is that it is then up to the people themselves to decide these issues.

People want more wildlife areas for aesthetic appreciation or recreational enjoyment? The greater demand for these things, as expressed in the prices that consumers are willing to pay, increases the profitability for land and resource owners to use less of what they own for other purposes and instead shift their resources into these more highly valued uses. If owners of land and resources most attractive for these purposes fail to do so, they will miss out on the higher income they could be earning. If an increased demand for housing and arts and crafts brings about an increased rate of deforestation, the remaining forests not yet touched by the woodchopper's ax will rise in price because of their increasing scarcity. This creates incentives on the part of forest owners to think ahead and replant trees at a greater rate, so the higher profits can be reaped in the future through harvesting or through other uses valued by consumers. If urban areas begin to encroach on areas of natural beauty—and if members of the society value them enough to be willing to pay for their preservation—the market will see to it that ownership of these areas passes into the hands of these people because that is where the greatest monetary return is expected.

Where are pollution problems, ecological imbalances, and assaults on areas of natural beauty taking place? Invariably, they are taking place in areas in society in which private property rights have not been permitted or have not been clearly delineated. No one knows for certain "what is mine and what is thine." In many of these areas, the resources in question are either in a no-man's-land of non-ownership or they are under the jurisdiction of the government. Non-ownership always produces what is known as "the tragedy of the commons." Where there is no owner, there is no cost for excessive misuse of a resource. And when no one directly feels the cost—in the form of lost income or depleted resale value—then everyone who has access to that ownerless resource will try to get as much out of it as is possible before others do.

Where property rights are not clearly specified, people will often act in ways that do not take into consideration the full effect and cost upon others. Resources and land are wrongly or excessively used because the users do not have to weigh or pay for the consequences of their actions upon others. This is the source of practically all the pollution problems that are cause for concern today.[43] By politicizing environmental problems, interventionists undermine the market's rational and reasonable mechanisms for finding out what people really value and what they are really willing to pay for. Special interests who lobby the state for environmental regulation are interested in getting what they want at the expense of others—others to whom they are unwilling to pay the real market price for the desired land and resources. Instead, they use the government to get what they want at below full market price through interventionist methods of coercion.[44]

The third type of public interest pleading argues that "public goods" are desirable products and services that are not adequately provided by the free market because it is simply not possible to exclude nonpayers from benefiting from its provision. This "free rider" dilemma means that private profit-seekers will undersupply the product or service in question. Popular examples are streets, highways, and lighthouses. Sometimes education is also listed as a public good benefiting the interests of the nation or community. And, of course, it is easy to conclude that all supposed public goods should be provided by the government.[45]

A closer examination of these examples shows that there is no logical reason why such goods and services cannot be supplied by the free market.[46] If a development corporation undertakes the construction of a residential community, it will clearly be in its own interest to construct a road system leading to and through the area. Access has a direct impact on the prospective value of the homes put up for sale. At the same time, the development corporation has incentives to include facilities such as playgrounds, swimming pools, recreational and shopping areas. Purchasing a home in this "proprietary community" would involve contracting for the provision of such "public services." The development corporation would lease out the stores in the shopping areas and maintain the roads, the street lighting, and other amenities that would make the area attractive, convenient, and desirable as a place to live.[47]

The same principle is inherent in the "condominium" concept in which the owners of the apartments pay a fee to the building owner for maintenance and security. It is also inherent in the concept of the "shopping mall," which the builder wants to make attractive and safe. Malls are usually surrounded by large parking areas with easy access to nearby roads and highways. Parking, restrooms, drinking fountains, benches, paging, and security surveillance are free. In traditional downtown areas, it is equally imaginable that if streets and sidewalks could be privatized there would be incentives for the owners to maintain them in good order, receiving fees from adjacent stores for providing this service. Generally speaking, streets and highways can easily be supplied with the same profit incentives. Suppliers would receive tolls in exchange for access. Unlike the present system under which the government supplies most streets and highways for "free" (i.e., on the basis of taxation) with open access for all drivers, private roads could offer "peak" and "off-peak" toll rates that would diminish highway congestion through a system of price rationing.[48] (Movie theaters and restaurants have rationed access in this way, respectively, with different matinee and evening ticket prices for movie attendance and different lunch and dinner menu prices.) Furthermore, roads and highways would also be constructed where the market demonstrates people desire to live, work, and play, and not where bureaucrats and city planners think they ought to be.[49]

The Individual, Morality, and the State

In 1936, Swiss economist and political scientist William E. Rappard delivered a lecture in Philadelphia on "The Relation of the Individual to the State." Looking back at the trend of political and economic events in the nineteenth and twentieth centuries, he explained:

> The revolutions at the end of the eighteenth century . . . were essentially revolts of the individual against the traditional state—expressions of his desire to emancipate himself from the ties and inhibitions which the traditional state had imposed on him. . . . [A]fter the rise of individualism, which one may define as the emancipation of the individual from the state, we had the rise of democracy, which one may define as the subjection of the state to the will of the individual. In the latter half of the nineteenth century and up to the present day, the individual, having emancipated himself from the state

and having subjected the state to his will, has furthermore demanded of the state that it serve his material needs. Thereby he has complicated the machinery of the state to such a degree that he has again fallen under subjection to it and he has been threatened with losing control over it. . . . [T]he individual has increasingly demanded of the state services which the state is willing to render. Thereby, however, he has been led to return to the state an authority over himself which it was the main purpose of the revolutions in the beginning of the nineteenth century to shake and to break.[50]

And looking back at the early American experience, Professor Rappard emphasized that:

[N]o one can possibly have read either the [constitutional] debates [of 1787] or the famous state papers of the Federalists without realizing that the Fathers of your Constitution were essentially animated by the desire to free the individual from the state. I believe you went farther in that direction than anyone had ever gone in the past. And your present Constitution bears the trace of this intransigent, almost ruthless, desire of the individual to free himself from the authority of the state. . . . I do not think that anyone who has seriously studied the origin of the Constitution of the United States will deny that it is an essentially individualistic document, inspired by the suspicion that the state is always, or always tends to be, dictatorial.[51]

Reflecting upon the trends he observed in the United States in the New Deal era of the 1930s, Professor Rappard concluded: "The individual demanding that the state provide him with every security has thereby jeopardized his possession of that freedom for which his ancestors fought and bled."

Is Soviet-style central planning now in the ash heap of history? Yes. Are masses of people in the West willing to walk in blind, lockstep obedience to fascist demagogues in torchlight parades? No. And hopefully neither form of totalitarianism will ever again cast its dark collectivist shadow over the West. However, six decades after Professor Rappard's observations about statist trends in America and around the world, Western democracies are still enveloped in the tight grip of the interventionist state. Private property increasingly exists only on paper.[52] And with the abridgment of property rights has come the abridgment of all the other individual liberties upon which a free society is based.[53] Our lives are supervised, regulated, controlled, directed, and overseen by the state. Look around in any direction of our economic and social lives and try to find even one corner of our existence free from some form of direct or indirect government intrusion into our personal and interpersonal affairs. It is practically impossible to find such a corner. Our lives are not our own. They are the property of the state. We are the tools and the victims of public policies that are intended to construct brave new worlds concocted by intellectual and political elites who still dream the utopian dream that they know better than the people themselves how their lives should be lived.[54]

Acts of Coercion

Today, it is not free market forces but political directives that most often influence what goods and services are produced, where and how they are produced, and for what purposes they may be used. Pick up any product in any store anywhere in the United States and you will discover that hundreds of federal and state regulations have actually determined the methods by which it has been manufactured, its quality and content, its packaging and terms of sale, and the conditions under which it may be "safely" used by the purchaser. Buy a tract of land or a building and you will be trapped in a spider's web of restrictions on how you may use, improve, or sell it. Every facet of our lives is now subject to the whims of the state.

In an environment in which "public policy" determines individual lives and fortunes, in which social and economic life has become politicized, it is not surprising that many Americans have turned their attention to politics to improve their market position and relative income share. Legalized coercion has become the method by which they get ahead in life. And make no mistake about it: Every income transfer, every tariff or import quota, every business subsidy, every regulation or prohibition on who may compete or how a product may be produced and marketed, and every restraint on the use and transfer of property is an act of coercion. Political force is interjected into what would otherwise be a system of peaceful and voluntary transactions.

Over time, interventionism blurs the distinction between what is moral and what is not. In ordinary life, most people take for granted that certain forms of conduct are permissible while others are not. These are the Golden Rules they live by. Government's task in society is to enforce and protect these rules, which, as I have already indicated, are summarized in two basic principles:

1. Neither force nor fraud shall be practiced in dealings with others.
2. The rights and property of others must be respected.

In the moral order that is the free market economy, these principles are the wellspring of honesty and trust. Without them, America is threatened with ultimate ruin—with a war of all-against-all in the pursuit of plunder. When individuals began to ask government to do things for them, rather than merely secure rights and property, they began asking government to violate other's rights and property for their benefit. Their demands on government have been rationalized by intellectuals and social engineers who have persuaded them that what they wanted but did not have was due to the greed, exploitation, and immorality of others. Basic morality and justice have been transcended in the political arena in order to take from the "haves" and give to the "have nots." Theft through political means has become the basis of a "higher" morality—social justice, which is supposed to remedy the alleged injustices of the free market economy.

Moral Bankruptcy

But once the market became politicized in this manner, morality began to degenerate. Increasingly, the only way to survive in society is to resort to the same types of political methods for gain as others are using or to devise ways to evade controls and regulations. More and more people have been drawn into the arena of

political intrigue and manipulation or violation of the law for economic gain. Human relationships and the political process have
become increasingly corrupted. In the 1920s, Mises explained a
crucial aspect of this corruption of morality and law:

> By constantly violating criminal laws and moral decrees
> [people] lose the ability to distinguish between right and
> wrong, good and bad. The merchant who began by violating
> foreign exchange controls, import and export restrictions,
> price ceilings, etc., easily proceeds to defraud his partners.
> The decay of business morals . . . is the inevitable concomitant
> of the regulations imposed on trade.[55]

Mises was, of course, repeating the lesson that French classical economist Frederic Bastiat had attempted to teach in the 1850s
in his famous essay "The Law."[56] When the state becomes the vio-
lator of liberty and property rather than its guarantor, it debases
respect for all law. Society develops an increasing disrespect and
disregard for what the law demands. They view the law as the agent
for immorality in the form of legalized plunder for the benefit of
some at the expense of others. And this same disrespect and disregard sooner or later starts to creep into dealings between individuals. Society verges on the brink of lawlessness, and the attitude
grows that "anything goes" in human relationships.

Bastiat predicted the moral bankruptcy that has been brought
on by the interventionist state. But are we condemned to continue down this path of moral and political corruption? Many
thoughtful observers shake their heads and conclude that the
answer is "yes." But it is worth recalling that, in 1951, Mises wrote
an essay called "Trends Can Change." He was replying to those
who despaired over the trend toward socialist central planning. At
the time, the situation did seem irreversible; political, economic,
and social trends all seemed to be heading in the direction of
comprehensive collectivism:

> One of the cherished dogmas implied in contemporary
> fashionable doctrines is the belief that tendencies of social
> evolution as manifested in the recent past will prevail in the

future too. Any attempt to reverse or even to stop a trend is doomed to failure. . . . The prestige of this myth is so enormous that it quells any opposition. It spreads defeatism among those who do not share the opinion that everything which comes later is better than what preceded, and are fully aware of the disastrous effects of all-round planning, i.e., totalitarian socialism. They too meekly submit to what, the pseudo-scholars tell them, is inevitable. It is this mentality of passively accepting defeat that has made socialism triumph in many European countries and may very soon make it conquer in this country [the United States] too. . . . Now trends of evolution can change, and hitherto they almost always have changed. But they changed only because they met firm opposition. The prevailing trend toward what Hilaire Belloc called the servile state will certainly not be reversed if nobody has the courage to attack its underlying dogmas.[57]

The trend toward totalitarian socialism *was* reversed. It was reversed by its own inherent unworkability. It was reversed by the faith of millions of people in the Soviet bloc who would not give up the dream of freedom and by a courageous few in those countries who were willing to risk imprisonment or their lives to make freedom a reality. And it was reversed by friends of freedom in the West who helped prevent its triumph in their homelands and who provided an intellectual defense of liberty and the free market.

Interventionism in America in the late twentieth century is a trend that can also be reversed. Its own inherent unworkability and strangulation of the wealth-creating mechanisms of the market has already started the reversal process. But that is not enough. We must rekindle our belief in and desire for freedom. And we have to speak out and refute the rationales for interventionism. We need to share with our fellow citizens a clear and persuasive vision of the free society and the unhampered market economy. If we succeed, the great trend of the twenty-first century will be toward greater individual freedom, an expanding global marketplace, and rising standards of living for all. That future can be ours, if only we have the courage to defend freedom and oppose the interventionist dogmas of our time.

Notes

[1]Ludwig von Mises, "Changes in American Economic Policy," *Industrial Club* (November 18, 1926).

[2]Ibid.

[3]For a comparison of the similarities between New Deal America and Nazi Germany in the 1930s, see Robert Skidelsky, *The Road From Serfdom: The Economic and Political Consequences of the End of Communism* (New York: Viking Penguin, 1996), 60–63; for an excellent contemporary account of the statist aspects of American economic policy in the 1930s, see A. S. J. Baster, *The Twilight of American Capitalism: An Economic Interpretation of the New Deal* (London: P. S. King & Son, 1937); also John T. Flynn, "Whose Child Is the NRA?" [1934] in *Forgotten Lessons: Selected Essays by John T. Flynn* (Irvington-on-Hudson, NY: Foundation for Economic Education, 1995); and for an overview of the economic thinking of those involved in Roosevelt's administration, see William J. Barber, *Designs within Disorder: Franklin D. Roosevelt, the Economists, and the Shaping of American Economic Policy, 1933–1945* (New York: Cambridge University Press, 1996).

[4]Ludwig von Mises, *Critique of Interventionism: Inquiries into the Economic Policy and the Economic Ideology of the Present* [1929] (Irvington-on-Hudson, NY: Foundation for Economic Education, 1996), xi.

[5]Ibid., 1.

[6]Mises, *Critique of Interventionism*, 2–3; see also Thomas Nixon Carver, *The Present Economic Revolution in the United States* (London: George Allen & Unwin, 1926), 5–6.

[7]Robert Skidelsky, *John Maynard Keynes: Hopes Betrayed, 1883–1920* (London: Macmillan, 1983); *John Maynard Keynes: The Economist as Saviour, 1920–1937* (London: Macmillan, 1992).

[8]Robert Skidelsky, ed. *Russia's Stormy Path to Reform* (London: Social Market Foundation, 1995).

[9]Robert Skidelsky, *The Road from Serfdom: The Economic and Political Consequences of the End of Communism* (New York: Viking Penguin, 1996).

[10]Oskar Morgenstern, *The Limits of Economics* [1934] (London: William Hodge and Co., 1937), 1; and Ludwig von Mises, *Human Action, A Treatise on Economics* [1949] (Irvington-on-Hudson, NY: Foundation for Economic Education, 4th ed., 1996), 718: "The system of interventionism or of the hampered market economy . . . does not want to eliminate the market altogether. It wants production and consumption to develop along lines different from those prescribed by an unhampered market, and it wants to achieve its aims by injecting into the working of the market orders, commands, and prohibitions for whose enforcement the police power and its apparatus of violent compulsion and coercion stand ready."

[11]Cf., Mises, *Human Action*, 719: "It is important to remember that government interference always means either violent action or the threat of such action. . . . Government is in the last resort the employment of armed men, of policemen, gendarmes, soldiers, prison guards, and hangmen. The essential feature of government is the enforcement of its decrees by beating, killing, and imprisoning. Those who ask for more government interference are asking ultimately for more compulsion and less freedom." See also Murray N. Rothbard, *Power and Market: Government and the Economy* (Menlo Park: Institute for Humane Studies, 1970), 9–11; Sanford Ikeda, *Dynamics of the Mixed Economy: Toward a Theory of Interventionism* (New York: Routledge, 1997), 35. Professor Ikeda's careful and detailed analysis of interventionism from an Austrian School point of view was only made available to me after the present paper was nearly complete and, therefore, I could not incorporate into my own thoughts on the nature and problems of interventionism and public policy any of the valuable insights he develops in his book. His short essay, "Interventionism," in Peter J. Boettke, ed., *The Elgar Companion to Austrian Economics* (Brookfield, VT: Edward Elgar Publishing, 1994), 345–51, offers a very brief summary of some of his arguments. Also worth consulting is his "Commentary" on "Regulation as a Process," in Richard M. Ebeling, ed., *Austrian Economics: Perspectives on the Past and Prospects for the Future*, Champions of Freedom, Vol. 17 (Hillsdale, MI: Hillsdale College Press, 1991), 291–301.

[12]See James M. Buchanan, *Property as a Guarantor of Liberty* (Brookfield, VT: Edward Elgar Publishing, 1993). On the history and general importance of private property rights, see Gottfried Dietze, *In Defense of Property* (Baltimore: Johns Hopkins University Press, 1963); see also Samuel L. Blumenfeld, ed., *Property in a Humane Economy* (LaSalle, IL: Open Court, 1974).

[13]Mises, *Human Action*, 159–66.

[14]Adam Smith, *The Wealth of Nations* [1776] (New York: Modern Library, 1936), 14.

[15]Mises, *Human Action*, 257–397; and Murray N. Rothbard, *Man, Economy and State: A Treatise on Economic Principles*, Vol. 2 [1962] (Los Angeles: Nash Publishing, 1970), 463–501.

[16]Ludwig von Mises, *Socialism, an Economic and Sociological Analysis* [1922] (Indianapolis: Liberty Classics, [3rd rev. ed., 1951] 1981), 30–32; see also John Bates Clark, *The Philosophy of Wealth* [1887] (New York: Augustus M. Kelley Publishers, 1967), 38–39: "The individual man . . . produces for the market. Every producer is serving the world, and the world is serving every consumer. . . . Society holds two distinct relations toward every man; it is the object of his efforts; he is the object of its efforts. He produces for the general market; it is his study to ascertain a public want, and to create to supply it. He buys from the general market; he informs himself con-

cerning the goods of many producers, and buys wherever the things offered are adapted in quality and price to his necessities."

[17]In its modern standard form, the conditions for a state of "perfect competition" to be present was first formalized by Frank H. Knight, *Risk, Uncer-
tainty, and Profit* [1921] (New York: Kelley & Millman, Inc. 1957), Part 2
on "Perfect Competition," 51–194; however, several years before publishing this book, in an article on "Neglected Factors in the Problem of Normal Interest," *Quarterly Journal of Economics* (February 1916), 283, Knight
referred to "the impossible conditions of ideally perfect competition,
where time and space were annihilated and universal omniscience pre-
vailed." See also Helmut Arndt, *Economic Theory vs. Economic Reality* (East
Lansing: Michigan State University Press, 1984), 37–65.

[18]See, for example, Ronald H. Coase, *The Firm, the Market, and the Law* (University of Chicago Press, 1988).

[19]See, for example, George J. Stigler, "The Economics of Information"
[1961] in *The Organization of Industry* (University of Chicago Press, 1968),
171–90.

[20]Friedrich A. Hayek, "The Meaning of Competition" [1946] in *Individualism and Economic Order* (University of Chicago Press, 1948), 92–106.

[21]For a detailed critique of many of the assumptions that are the foundation of neoclassical equilibrium theory that is written by a prominent Austrian School economist of the interwar period, see Hans Mayer, "The
Cognitive Value of Functional Theories of Price" [1932] in Israel M.
Kirzner, ed., *Classics in Austrian Economics*, Vol. 2 (London: William Picker-
ing, 1994), 55–168; and for a modern reformulation, see Robin Cowan
and Mario J. Rizzo, "The Genetic–Causal Tradition and Modern Economic Theory," *Kyklos*, Vol. 49, No. 3 (1996), 273–317.

[22]For a critical analysis of the neoclassical conception of competition from
a modern Austrian School point of view, see Dominick T. Armentano,
Antitrust and Monopoly: Anatomy of a Policy Failure (New York: John Wiley &
Sons, 1982), 13–48; see also Israel M. Kirzner, "The Driving Force of the
Market: The Idea of 'Competition' in Contemporary Economic Theory
and in the Austrian Theory of the Market Process" in Richard M. Ebeling,
ed., *Austrian Economics: Perspectives on the Past and Prospects for the Future*,
Champions of Freedom, Vol. 17 (Hillsdale, MI: Hillsdale College Press,
1991), 139–60; and Mark Addleson, "Competition," in Peter J. Boettke,
ed., *The Elgar Companion to Austrian Economics* (Brookfield, VT: Edward
Elgar Publishing, 1994), 96–102.

[23]For Austrian School criticisms of such policy proposals, see Stephen C.
Littlechild, *The Fallacy of the Mixed Economy: An 'Austrian' Critique of Conven-
tional Economics and Government Policy* (San Francisco: Cato Institute, 1979);
W. Duncan Reekie, *Markets, Entrepreneurs, and Liberty: An Austrian View of
Capitalism* (New York: St. Martin's Press, 1984); and D. T. Armentano,

Antitrust: The Case for Repeal (Washington, DC: Cato Institute, 1986). For a critical analysis of the "operational" assumptions underlying many interventionist policy proposals, see Robert Formaini, *The Myth of Scientific Public Policy* (New Brunswick, NJ: Transaction Books, 1990).

[24]For summaries of the ideas of the Austrian School economists in contrast to the ideas of other schools of economic thought, see Ludwig M. Lachmann, "The Significance of the Austrian School of Economics in the History of Ideas," [1966] in Richard M. Ebeling, ed., *Austrian Economics: A Reader*, Champions of Freedom, Vol. 18 (Hillsdale, MI: Hillsdale College Press, 1991), 17–39; Richard M. Ebeling, "The Significance of Austrian Economics in Twentieth-Century Economic Thought," in Richard M. Ebeling, ed., *Austrian Economics: Perspectives on the Past and Prospects for the Future*, op. cit., 1–40; and Israel M. Kirzner, "Entrepreneurial Discovery and the Competitive Market Process: An Austrian Approach," *Journal of Economic Literature* (March 1997), 60–85.

[25]Friedrich A. Hayek, "Competition as a Discovery Procedure," [1968] in *New Studies in Philosophy, Politics, Economics and the History of Ideas* (University of Chicago Press, 1978), 179–90; see also E. G. West, *Adam Smith and Modern Economics* (Brookfield, VT: Edward Elgar Publishing Co., 1990), 21–23.

[26]See Friedrich A. Hayek, "The Use of Knowledge in Society," [1945] in *Individualism and Economic Order*, 77–91. On the classical economists' view of the market economy in comparison to the view of most twentieth century economists, see Richard M. Ebeling, "How Economics Became the Dismal Science," in Richard M. Ebeling, ed., *Economic Education: What Should We Learn About the Free Market?* Champions of Freedom, Vol. 22 (Hillsdale, MI: Hillsdale College Press, 1994), 51–81.

[27]See Mises, *Human Action*, 200–217, on the meaning and significance of economic calculation.

[28]The logic and process of such entrepreneurial "discovery" has been the theme of most of the writings of Israel M. Kirzner; see *Competition and Entrepreneurship* (University of Chicago Press, 1973); *Perception, Opportunity, and Profit: Studies in the Theory of Entrepreneurship* (University of Chicago Press, 1979); *Discovery and the Capitalist Process* (University of Chicago Press, 1985); *Discovery, Capitalism, and Distributive Justice* (New York: Blackwell, Publishers, 1989); and *The Meaning of Market Process: Essays in the Development of Modern Austrian Economics* (New York: Routledge, 1992).

[29]Friedrich A. Hayek, *Law, Legislation, and Liberty*, Vol. 2, "The Mirage of Social Justice" (University of Chicago Press, 1976), 115–20.

[30]See Norman P. Barry, *The Invisible Hand in Economics and Politics: A Study in the Two Conflicting Explanations of Society: End-States and Processes* (London: Institute of Economic Affairs, 1988).

[31]Eugen von Böhm-Bawerk, *Capital and Interest* [1914], Vol. 1 (South Holland, IL: Libertarian Press, 1959), 241–321; Böhm-Bawerk, "Unresolved Contradiction in the Marxian System" [1896] in *Shorter Classics* (South Holland, IL: Libertarian Press, 1962), 201–302; also H. W. B. Joseph, *The Labour Theory of Value in Karl Marx* (London: Oxford University Press, 1923).

[32]The classic essay on this theme is Eugen von Böhm-Bawerk, "Control or Economic Law," [1914] in *Shorter Classics*, 139–99.

[33]On the economic effects of coerced collective bargaining, see W. H. Hutt, *The Theory of Collective Bargaining, 1930–1975* (London: Institute of Economic Affairs, 1975); Hutt, *The Strike-Threat System: The Economic Consequences of Collective Bargaining* (New Rochelle, NY: Arlington House, 1973); Sylvester Petro, *The Labor Policy of the Free Society* (New York: Ronald Press, 1957); Gustavo R. Velsaso, *Labor Legislation from an Economic Point of View* (Indianapolis: Liberty Fund, 1973); Morgan O. Reynolds, *Power and Privilege: Labor Unions in America* (New York: Universe Books, 1984); and Howard Dickman, *Industrial Democracy in America: Ideological Origins of National Labor Relations Policy* (LaSalle, IL: Open Court, 1987).

[34]Hayek, *Law, Legislation and Liberty*, Vol. 2, 62–100.

[35]Students sometimes resent the fact that their grade is solely dependent upon on how well they have "delivered the goods," i.e., answered the questions on an exam with correct and complete answers, and not on the basis of how "hard" they have studied. It bothers some students that someone for whom the material "comes easy" gets an "A," while someone who studied for long hours is "given" a lower grade.

[36]Allen G. B. Fisher, "More Stabilization: Less Stability," *Kyklos*, Vol. 1, No. 1 (1947), 3–4.

[37]Allen G. B. Fisher, "The Economic Implications of Material Progress," *International Labor Review* (July 1935), 7–8; on this general theme, see Allen G. B. Fisher, *The Clash of Progress and Security* [1935] (New York: Augustus M. Kelley, Publishers, 1966).

[38]See Mises, *Human Action*, 289–94 and Mises, "Profit and Loss" [1951] in *Planning for Freedom* (South Holland, IL: Libertarian Press, 4th rev. ed., 1980), 108–50, on the nature and role of profit and loss in the free market economy.

[39]Edwin Cannan, *An Economist's Protest* (London: P. S. King & Son, 1927), vii-viii.

[40]Mises, *Human Action*, 599–600.

[41]This theme is developed in great detail in Dwight R. Lee and Richard B. McKenzie, *Failure and Progress: The Bright Side of the Dismal Science* (Washington, DC: Cato Institute, 1993).

[42] See Edwin Cannan, *Economic Scares* (London: P. S. King & Son, 1933), 21–41.

⁴³Mises, *Human Action*, 654–61

⁴⁴See Richard L. Stroup and John A. Baden, *Natural Resources: Bureaucratic Myths and Environmental Management* (San Francisco: Pacific Institute for Public Policy Research, 1983); Walter E. Block, ed., *Economics and the Environment: A Reconciliation* (Vancouver: Fraser Institute, 1990); Terry L. Anderson and Donald R. Leal, *Free Market Environmentalism* (Boulder: Westview Press, 1991); Roy E. Cordato, *Welfare Economics and Externalities in an Open Ended Universe: A Modern Austrian Perspective* (Boston: Kluwer Academic Press, 1992); Joseph Bast, Peter J. Hill, and Richard C. Rue, *Eco-Sanity: A Common-Sense Guide to Environmentalism* (Lanham, MD: Madison Books, 1994); Terry L. Anderson, ed., *Breaking Environmental Policy Gridlock* (Stanford: Hoover Institution, 1997).

⁴⁵A recent example of such a rationale for subsidized public education is Charles Murray, *What It Means to be a Libertarian: A Personal Interpretation* (New York: Broadway Books, 1997), 90–101; however, on the advantages of a fully privatized system of education, see Sheldon Richman, *Separating School and State: How to Liberate America's Families* (Fairfax, VA: Future of Freedom Foundation, 1994).

⁴⁶For a refutation of the claim that lighthouses are an obvious public good, see Ronald H. Coase, "The Lighthouse in Economics," [1974] in *The Firm, The Market, and the Law*, 187–213.

⁴⁷See Spencer Heath, *Citadel, Market, and Altar* (Baltimore: Science of Society Foundation, 1957), and Spencer MacCullum, *The Art of Community* (Menlo Park: Institute for Humane Studies, 1970); on the general refutation of the public goods argument along these lines, see Fred Foldvary, *Public Goods and Private Communities: The Private Provision of Social Services* (Brookfield, VT: Edward Elgar Publishing, 1994).

⁴⁸See John Hibbs, *Transport Without Politics . . . ?* (London: Institute of Economic Affairs, 1982); Eammon Butler, ed., *Roads and the Private Sector* (London: Adam Smith Institute, 1982); Gabriel Roth and Eammon Butler, *Private Roads Ahead* (London: Adam Smith Institute, 1982); see also Francis A. Walker, *Political Economy* (New York: Henry Holt and Co., 1888), 520: "Public roads and bridges also exhibit the socialistic character in a highly marked degree."

⁴⁹See Jane Jacobs, *The Death and Life of Great American Cities* (New York: Vintage Books, 1961).

⁵⁰William E. Rappard, "The Relation of the Individual to the State," *Annals of the American Academy of Political and Social Science* (January 1937), 215–18.

⁵¹Ibid.

⁵²See Richard A. Epstein, *Takings: Private Property and the Power of Eminent Domain* (Cambridge: Harvard University Press, 1985); and Mark L. Pollot, *Grand Theft and Petit Larceny: Property Rights in America* (San Francisco: Pacific Research Institute for Public Policy, 1993).

[53]See Bernard H. Siegan, *Economic Liberties and the Constitution* (University of Chicago Press, 1980).

[54]See Bertrand de Jouvenel, "The Attitude of Intellectuals to the Market Society," *The Owl* (January 1951), 19–27; and Thomas Sowell, *The Vision of the Anointed: Self-Congratulation as a Basis for Social Policy* (New York: Basic Books, 1995).

[55]Mises, *Critique of Interventionism*, 13.

[56]Frederic Bastiat, "The Law" [1850], *Selected Essays on Political Economy* (Princeton: D. Van Nostrand, 1964), 51–96.

[57]Ludwig von Mises, "Trends Can Change" [1951], *Planning for Freedom*, 173–74, 179.

SPENCER ABRAHAM

American Injustice: The Case for Legal Reform

Our legal system is broken. The United States has been transformed from a nation of friends and neighbors into a nation of actual and potential litigants. The separation of powers and the provisions of the Constitution have been defied by activist judges who prefer making laws to observing them and substituting their will for the will of the people. These are serious allegations, to be sure. What I would like to do here is briefly examine each and present the case for legal reform.

Frivolous Lawsuits

We should not keep people with genuine injuries and claims from seeking redress through the judicial process. But the damage being done by frivolous lawsuits is all too obvious. The current system hurts our economy and our competitiveness. Litigation adds 2.5 percent to the average cost of a new product in America; the figure is much higher for advanced technology and medical goods and services. One reputable research group reports that court costs, awards, and lost time cost our economy $132 billion in 1991 alone. Imagine how that figure has soared in recent years. We also pay for frivolous lawsuits through decreased innovation. According to a Gallup survey, one of every five small businesses decides not to introduce a new product or to improve an existing one because of fear of litigation.

The rules for playing the frivolous lawsuit game are quite predictable. *The first rule is to sue anyone in sight, no matter how minimally connected they are to the injury.* Just to give you a case in point, a man recently attended a boxing match, had too much to drink, got into an altercation, and fell down a flight of stairs. He died as a result of his injuries. Unbelievably, one of the defendants named in the suit brought by his family was Ticketmaster, the company that had issued tickets to the boxing match.

The second rule is to claim that the defendant should protect the plaintiff against injury regardless of circumstances. It doesn't matter if the plaintiff is negligent or willfully disregards proper safety procedures. In the case of *Piper Aircraft* v. *Cleveland*, a man bought an airplane and decided to remove the pilot's seat and attempt to handle the controls from the back seat. The plane crashed and he was killed. His family sued Piper Aircraft and collected a $1 million judgment. His death was a tragedy, but to claim that the company that built his plane was to blame is simply wrong. It also perverts the traditional definition of legal responsibility, making virtually every manufacturer liable for injuries that occur through deliberate misuse of a product.

The third rule is to establish any conceivable level of negligence against the party with "deep pockets," so that party can be forced to pay all of the damages. This is known as the doctrine of "joint and several liability," which currently prevails in our legal system. It means that if a defendant is only 1 percent negligent, he can still be held responsible for 100 percent of the damages.

Several years ago, Walt Disney World found out how unjust this doctrine can be. A young couple decided to play "bumper cars" on the Grand Prix go-cart track. Now those of you who have been to the Magic Kingdom know how difficult it is to do this. The cars are spaced so they cannot touch each other, and they cannot go more than about seven miles per hour. But at the very end of the track, where the drivers disembark, there is a momentary window of opportunity in which a determined and reckless driver can crash into the car ahead. Apparently that's what happened in this case. The young man was finally able to do what he had repeatedly tried to do and crashed into his fiancée's car. She was injured, and she went to court. The jury found that the young man was 85 percent negligent. The young woman was 14 percent negligent. And Walt Disney World was 1 percent negligent. Guess who ended up paying the entire judgment? Disney, of course, since it had the deepest pockets.

The fourth and last rule is to sue in states or in jurisdictions where punitive damage awards have typically been astronomical. Any lawyer can tell you: Where you sue sometimes makes as much if not more difference than who you sue and why. There are particular courts and judges that are notorious for awarding millions of dollars to the plaintiffs in frivolous lawsuits. But they are never forced to pay the price for their bias.

Changing the Rules

We need to change the rules in the lawsuit game. The first rule change is limiting punitive damages. Originally intended to be a rare punishment imposed only on convicted defendants who had acted with an unusual degree of recklessness or viciousness, punitive damages have become increasingly common and, in many instances, the dollar amounts involved have been astronomical. A cap would permit plaintiffs to recover their due—full compensation for true losses and injuries—while discouraging profit-seeking lawsuits and the use of punitive damage claims to frighten defendants into agreeing to out-of-court settlements. It would also free up the court calendar and lessen the huge burden litigation has placed on our economy.

The second rule change is replacing joint and several liability with "proportionate liability." This would lessen the unfairness and expense of the current system in which defendants with "deep pockets" must involuntarily serve as insurers for everyone who crosses their path. Under proportionate liability, plaintiffs would no longer be able to force defendants with the most money to pay just because they can.

The third rule change is reforming "conflict of law" provisions that govern lawsuits between parties from different states. In corporate cases, plaintiffs would be required to bring suit using the provisions of the state in which the defending company has the most employees. This would mean plaintiffs could not simply pick the state with the best (meaning the worst) record of high awards for frivolous lawsuits. And because states do tend to worry about such issues as competitiveness, attracting new businesses, and job creation, this rule change might actually lead them to improve their records.

Changing the Players

Beyond changing the rules, we also need to change some of the players. No substantive legal reform is possible without ridding the system of "judicial activists," that is, judges who act as legislators in the courtroom. The black-robed heirs of Solomon who sit on the bench today have a crucial role to play in our legal system. We should do nothing to bar them from determining the constitutionality of our laws. But we cannot allow them to make the law, which is exactly what many modern judges have been doing.

One recent example is provided by *U.S. Term Limits* v. *Thornton.* Now, not everyone agrees on whether there should be term limits for political office. But when the voters of a given state decide they want term limits, surely they should be able to give them a try. In a 1992 ballot initiative that commanded over 60 percent support, Arkansas voters adopted term limits for their U.S. senators and representatives. At the time, twenty-two states had adopted similar limits (twenty-one by direct vote). The Supreme Court struck down all congressional term limits laws in a five-to-four decision in 1995. The tortured logic of the majority was that the Constitution—which explicitly allows states to decide a number of key questions about federal elections—forbids them from limiting the terms of their representatives in the federal government. Where did the Supreme Court find this prohibition? Not in the Constitution but in the implicit notion of "national sovereignty" and, ironically, in the people's right to decide who will represent them.

In *Romer* v. *Evans,* the Supreme Court held by a six-to-three vote in 1996 that the Constitution's equal protection clause prevents the states from outlawing special legal protections for homosexuals. Now, leaving aside valid questions about the morality of this "alternative lifestyle" and the need to legally protect it, we can say with absolute certainty that this is an issue on which the Constitution is totally silent. Some states have adopted legislation regarding homosexuals; some have not. But it is virtually impossible to conclude that the Constitution constrains them from doing so. Impossible for everyone to conclude, that is, but certain judicial activists who preside over the highest court of the land.

Amazed as they would be by the *Term Limits* and *Romer* decisions, the Founding Fathers would be struck dumb by the recent California case in which a district court judge struck down the California Civil Rights Initiative (CCRI). In this case, the judge concluded that the ballot initiative—which outlawed discrimination and preference on the basis of race or sex in public employment (including education and contracting) and which was approved by 54 percent of California voters—should not be allowed to go into effect because it allegedly violates the equal protection clause. Once again, there is room for disagreement about the merits of the initiative, but not about its constitutionality. CCRI is true, in both the letter and spirit of the law, to the equal protection clause. Worse yet, invalidating this kind of ballot initiative destroys the very foundations of our republic. It destroys local and state government. It destroys communities by taking disputes out of the realm of public debate and out of the democratic process. It destroys Americans' confidence that their votes count. And it destroys constitutional limits on judicial power.

Restoring Limits

The cases I have cited are not the only ones in which judicial activism should concern us. They are simply the most recent and striking examples of how the courts and, in many instances, lone judges have overruled the democratic process and twisted the Constitution to serve their own ends. How then do we restore constitutional limits on judicial power? Let me address this question by examining one specific target area where reform has already begun to change the rules and the players in the judicial activism game. When I was elected to the U.S. Senate in 1994, I discovered that the federal courts had virtually taken over, in whole or in part, the administration of prisons in thirty-nine states. This included three hundred of the nation's largest penal institutions. In many jurisdictions, judicial decrees had led to skyrocketing operating costs, dramatically reduced punitive and deterrent effects of sentencing, and the early release of literally thousands of dangerous criminals. Moreover, these decrees had precipitated an avalanche of frivolous prisoner lawsuits. Although the vast majority were found to be without merit (over 99 percent in the Ninth Circuit and at least 95 percent in all jurisdictions nationwide), these lawsuits were taking up enormous amounts of time, money, and manpower—precious resources that could be better spent on incarcerating offenders. On the question of money alone, the National Association of Attorneys General estimated that the typical annual cost of prisoner lawsuits exceeded $80 million.

In 1995, 65,000 prisoner lawsuits were filed in federal court. That is more than the total number of criminal prosecutions in all federal jurisdictions for the same year. Yet in Michigan, for example, prisons had to be routinely monitored to determine:

— how warm the food was;
— how bright the lights were;
— whether there were electrical outlets in each cell;
— whether windows were inspected and up to code;
— whether prisoners' hair was cut by licensed barbers; and
— whether air and water temperatures were "comfortable."

Such micromanagement might be understandable if a court had ever found that Michigan's prison system was in violation of the Constitution in any of these areas, or if conditions were inhumane, but this was not the case. No court had ever found that Michigan's prisons had violated the Constitution or any federal law in any of these areas. In addition, Michigan boasted the number-one training program for corrections officers. Its rate of prison violence was one of the lowest in the nation. It spent an average of $4,000 a year per prisoner for health care, including nearly $1,700 for mental health services. Nevertheless, complying with court orders, litigating over what they meant, and producing the reports necessary to keep individual judges satisfied had cost Michigan taxpayers hundreds of millions of dollars over the course of a decade.

While the judicial decrees imposed on Michigan were bad, there were worse. In some states, judges "cured" prison overcrowding by freeing dangerous criminals years before they had finished serving their time and by refusing to incarcerate certain types of criminals. One of the worst situations was in Philadelphia. For eight years, a single federal judge oversaw a "cap" program that released up to six hundred criminal defendants per week. This kept the prison population at what she considered an "appropriate level." It did not matter whether the defendants had one or more previous convictions or if these convictions had been for shoplifting or murder. If the charge giving rise to the current arrest was based on a "non-violent crime," the defendant could not be held in custody prior to his trial. Not surprisingly, thousands of the defendants who had been returned to the streets were rearrested for new crimes. In one 18-month period, there were rearrests for 79 murders; 959 robberies; 2,214 drug deals; 90 rapes; and 1,113 assaults. The citizens of Philadelphia lost faith in the ability of the legal system to protect them. The criminals, on the other hand, had every reason to believe that the system could not punish them.

In 1996, I helped author legislation that is the crucial first step toward restoring limits on judicial power and taking judicial activists out of the game. Already, there have been enormous positive changes as a result of the Prison Litigation Reform Act (PLRA):

— Lawsuits brought by inmates must meet stricter standards.
— Caps on attorney fees have been established in such cases.
— There must be proof of actual violations before judicial decrees regarding prison conditions can be issued.
— Courts must take the public's safety into serious consideration when decreeing changes in the operation of the criminal justice system.
— And in cases brought in federal court, only panels of three federal judges can order early release for defendants, and only as a last resort.

The PRLA has not undone all the damage caused by previous decisions. And it remains to be seen whether the courts will uphold key provisions. So far, the courts have been split. And a number of state statutes, passed in part in response to court orders about prisons, continue to dictate early prisoner releases. Much more needs to be done, but this single piece of legislation proves that we *can* change the rules and the players. We *can* contain the litigation explosion, curb judicial activism, and restore authority and safety to our penal system. We should not look to the PLRA as a cure-all but as a model for other reforms aimed at restoring American justice. By re-establishing responsibility under law to potential litigants, judges, and criminals, we can make our country once again a land of family, friends, and neighbors.

JOSEPH E. BROADUS

Property and Civil Liberty

Everyone knows that there are serious problems in our civil justice system. I do not wish to enumerate new complaints here. Instead, I plan to provide a little history and theory regarding the relationship between property and civil liberty.

Ultimately, the civil justice system has two objectives when it comes to property. The first is to recognize or define various property interests in a manner that makes them relatively certain and that encourages appropriate investment. The second is to provide for a fair and efficient method of resolving property disputes. The proper performance of these functions is critical for it provides the foundation for our entire economic order. Of course, we all know that a civil justice system has greater goals than the efficient allocation of material resources; it must also strive to settle disputes over personal injury and resolve conflicts between the individual and the state over issues of freedom. But what is also clear is the fact that the way in which the system achieves these goals is colored by the way it addresses property questions.

Once upon a time, property was seen as central to liberty. That is because there has never been—not now, not ever—a democratic order without it.[1] In the last generation, however, despite growing affluence at every level of society, property has fallen from its lofty pedestal. It is frequently regarded as a threat to, rather than a fountain of, liberty. Historically speaking, Americans have always been wary that extremes of wealth and poverty might distort the social and political order, but now they seem to distrust the very institution of property, and this has allowed for the weak-

ening property's protections under the law and the expansion of
state power

Nexus: Property, Liberty, Democracy

The Framers of the U.S. Constitution had some very definite, and
very traditional, notions about property. They regarded it, for example, as a shield between individuals and the will of the world.
They wanted to give legal expression to the centuries-old maxim
that a man's home is his castle; it is the place where the state cannot intervene, and it is his fortress, his refuge, and, quite literally,
his domain. That is why there are so many protections for property built into the Constitution and the Bill of Rights. But today, the
Framers' wisdom has been forgotten. Property is increasingly regarded as an anti-social force, as an expression of greed, and as a
source of social problems. And the state regularly forces its way
into virtually every home in the land.

    This new negative view of property has been introduced by
the liberal elites of our society.[2] These elites have "reconstructed,"
that is, rewritten, history to reflect their own present concerns
and biases. Specifically, they have rewritten it to make it appear as
if the old regime—the one based on limited government and a
strong defense of private property—concentrated wealth in the
hands of the few and condemned the many to poverty.[3] Property
rights only increased inequality and powerlessness. But under the
new regime known as the "modern administrative state," wealth
has been redistributed, the state has intervened to protect people
from their worst impulses, and greater equality and liberty have
been assured. Elites cast our entire national history in strictly evo-
lutionary terms: Only as private property rights have been curtailed and government powers have been expanded, have we seen
real Progress with a capital "P." Indeed, the bulwark of all liberty is
not property; it is the state. At the heart of this elitist view is a
fundamental shift in core concern. No longer is society dedicated, above all, to recognizing human accomplishment, creativity,
and virtue, and to providing opportunities for these things to flourish. No longer is the law based on respect for individual rights and
property rights. The new core concern for society and for the law

is protecting "groups" and "classes" against exploitation by property owners.[4]

Two traditions—property as a fountain of liberty and property as an enemy of equality and democracy—are thus locked in conflict. The first tradition is rooted in custom and the common law and assumes that individuals are best equipped to make good choices because they know their own situation and have command of their own destiny. The second tradition is rooted in liberal political theory and social engineering and assumes that "experts" should make choices for everyone because they are detached professionals supposedly untainted by greed, ignorance, personal ambition, or bias. The war between these competing traditions is essentially the cause of the crisis in our civil justice system. Elites have managed to substitute their vision of how we should live and treat one another for the Framers' vision and the historic traditions of our nation. They have done so through subtle changes in the language of the law that have shifted the emphasis from the protection of property and individual rights to the protection of "process" and the "public welfare."

What Is Property?

What is property? We usually think of property as a thing: a car, a building, or money in the bank. But there are many less tangible forms, from driveway easements to author's royalties and patents. And not all of these forms have direct cash-value equivalents. Properly understood, property is ultimately that which gives us the capacity to say two small words: "mine" and "no." Property is also distinguished by three elements: (1) an individual is able to decide how he will use it; (2) he is able to exclude others from using it; and (3) he has some reasonable expectation that others will respect his ownership. The system which ensures that all three of these elements are protected is the civil justice system.[5]

Why is property critical to liberty? The answer is immediately obvious in one sense. The ability to say "mine" and "no" builds a buffer between the owner and others. What is not as obvious is the fact that property is not just about the control or manipulation of things external to the self and in competition with others. *Every form of property is an extension of the physical self.* What do clothing and a house have in common? They are both substitutes for your skin because they protect you from the environment. What is a car? An extension of your feet for locomotion. Every conceivable bit of property is significant not just as an external thing you can control but as something that expands and extends your power and control—your ability to act independently. And this is why limits on property are so damaging: They are limits on the individual freedom to act.

To liberal elites, however, the old nexus between property and liberty is simply a false connection. They particularly enjoy denouncing the era in history when only property owners could vote and they characterize property as a villainous device for excluding the vast majority of citizens from influencing important political decisions. But why was property a requirement for the franchise? It was because it was widely feared that people without property lacked independence and that their votes would merely and always be additional votes for those on whom they were dependent. We can see this same fear behind the modern campaign finance reform movement, which presupposes that those with great wealth will dominate the political process by sheer ability to "buy" votes and politicians.

Law: Property, Liberty, and Change

One of the most impressive features of the twentieth century is the incredible rate of technological change. Innovation and invention are rapidly transforming the familiar patterns and features of our world. Even more dramatic is the mere presumption that there will be massive change. It is easy to forget that in the past most communities remained fairly stable in terms of technology. Big changes occurred not once a week or once a year, but once every decade or even every century. Today, however, sweeping change is treated not so much as a marvel but as something of an inconvenience, disrupting our daily patterns and forcing us to make new purchases in order to remain up-to-date. Change fails to startle us precisely because we expect it.

The other impressive feature of our age is the rate at which we write new laws and regulations—thousands upon thousands of pages a year. Historically, much of human behavior has been regulated by custom. Established patterns of behavior have persisted over generations. For more than two thousand years, one of the most critical processes was teaching the young the basic technologies of hunting and farming. In subsistence societies, a failure to follow these patterns led to disaster. The authority of the older generation was based on its mastery of the skills necessary for survival—skills that were handed down from prior generations and would be handed down to future generations. Only the seasons seemed to change. It was in this context that the basic outline of our laws was born. It was called the "common law." Its foundations went back beyond the memory of any living man, and they were assumed to be part of nature.

In this Old World, innovation was discouraged. It was risky. One bad crop could mean the extinction of an entire community. It was disruptive. Even when it resulted in a gain for the innovator, it would surely disrupt the lives of his neighbors. It was distracting. Living on the margin, there was little time to experiment. It was impolitic. New ways inspired envy and discontent and a call for new leadership. Naturally, this description is overly broad. It does, however, capture the flavor of much of traditional life over great periods of time. But in the New World known as America, the situation was entirely different. Change was a fact of life. The land, the soil, the crops—all presented new challenges. Americans consequently developed new attitudes about innovation that were unlike those shared by their European cousins. To Americans, innovation and survival were one. Traditional methods had to be re-evaluated, adapted, modified, or rejected. And American children, unburdened by the assumptions of the past, suddenly had an advantage over their parents; they could adapt better.

The great tie of common practices and a common life were broken by changes in agricultural life. Also dawning was a new industrial age—a new way of thinking, acting, and doing that would challenge the past and make the future an even greater unknown. What was once easy to know—the best practice for doing this-or-that—could no longer be solely the province of custom; expertise had to be developed and experimentation had to be tried. With this shift in behavioral practices came a shift in legal practices, too. The law had once assumed that old patterns were best. Its basic aim was to discern those practices and preserve them. The age of exploration, innovation, and industry changed everything. The law could no longer venerate past practice; instead it had to find ways to accommodate new and old.

Adjusting to Change

It is important to note that the law adjusts to change in two basic ways: legislatively and judicially. Legislative responses usually tend to arise from a comprehensive theory about a given situation and represent a comprehensive solution. An example is provided by one of the great perils of the Middle Ages: highway robbery. In England, the king decided that it was not enough to punish robbers; they must be deterred from robbing. So he issued an edict requiring that landowners whose property bordered the main roads must clear the land on either side for at least twenty feet of all of trees and shrubs. This new law created a safe zone; it restricted the ability of robbers to ambush travelers without warning. But it also placed a new burden on property. Landowners had to pay the expense of protecting all those who traveled on the King's Highway.[6] As for the robbers, they had to develop more ingenious ways of plying their trade. Then more laws were required to adapt to those new ways, and so on and so on. In our time, we can see the same cycle repeating itself when it comes to auto theft. Some years ago, increases in auto theft lead to the development of mandatory door locks as well as such options as car alarms and security codes. These innovations have prompted thieves to change their methods; their new *modus operandi* is "carjacking," a change in practice that circumvents locks and alarms because the passenger is still in his vehicle at the time that it is stolen. And carjacking is encouraging the passage of new laws designed to suppress the practice. In both examples, legislation is comprehensive. The theory of how to respond to the problem is developed in advance: Every landowner had to clear the land; every car had to have door locks.

Penalties for robbers and carjackers are also imposed according to a uniform set of laws. And in each case comprehensive legislation changes the nature of the property interest by imposing new and substantial burdens on property ownership.

The judicial method is largely *post hoc* to the legislative *ex ante*. It seeks to sort out the mess rather than prevent it from happening. It is also less comprehensive; it seeks to address specific disputes, working out the best solution for a particular case based on intense fact-gathering. The judicial method also stresses specific outcomes. It first emerged in the Old World when technology was relatively fixed. Over a long period of time and case by case, the courts catalogued the permissible and prohibited uses of property. Mostly, this work was achieved at the margin, defining where one use stopped and another commenced. Each property owner was presumed to have the right to exploit his property fully. The property, however, did not include the right to intrude on another's use of his own property. Frequently, the courts were involved in untangling competing claims of unlimited use. Usually, a violating use involved a physical invasion of another's property, as when water flooded land because a dam was built downstream. But the intrusion could also involve an expectation of use, as when a dam built upstream prevented water from reaching land downstream.

Judicial responses to problems and adjustments to change have tended to be conservative and incremental. Legislation can properly be far more dramatic. Following the Great Fire of London in 1666, a building code was enacted to govern the rebuilding of the city. Its provisions included requirements for proper spacing between buildings and for appropriate building materials to avoid future fires. The response was dynamic and comprehensive. The fire was a crisis, which suggested the need for an immediate rather an incremental response. The scale of the city itself was a problem. While each property owner had merely exploited his property in the traditionally permitted ways, the result was a disaster. The problem was not that any property owner had violated his duty to the others. The problem was the system; the city itself was dangerous. Perhaps, the judiciary—after repeated trials —could have emerged with appropriate rules for rebuilding the city. The risk, however, would have been repeated fires while the

searched was conducted. The legislature was simply better at responding to dynamic circumstances. It could envision a new pattern and set new rules for the future. It could respond to crisis, or
it could attempt to avoid conflict by projecting trends. Further, it
could change the basic ground rules by reflecting the changed
moral attitudes of the people. The risk, however, was that property could become problematic and that legislation would impose
too much on property owners.[7]

There has long been, therefore, both a natural tension and a
complimentary nature to the legislative and judicial processes. The
judiciary addresses individual and small group conflict under a
basically conservative pattern that values long-term patterns. The
legislature provides for dynamic response to systemwide problems
and encourages innovation. The legislature can play an increasingly important role where technology can swiftly produce change
of a scale and scope beyond normal judicial limits or where the
choice between competing uses requires a value judgment about
the future.

Obviously, a stable system of property and liberty in a complex society of rapid change requires an appropriate balance between legislative and judicial conflict resolution and policymaking.
The nature of our civil justice problem is a not-too-subtle breakdown in that distinction between legislative and judicial roles. Part
of the confusion is a side effect of our constitutional system of
checks and balances. The judiciary is often peopled by holdover
judges from an earlier regime either more conservative or more
liberal than the members of the legislature. When this happens,
the courts either tend to constitutionalize problems in order to
curtail change or devise theories to advance legislative agendas
beyond traditional limits. When the latter occurs, judges seem to
evolve doctrine out of thin air. Over the last century, in fact, the
courts have become the tools of the legislature. It doesn't matter
particularly if they are tools of the minority that is on the skids or
if they are the tools of the majority that is advancing an agenda by
clever craftsmanship. They are tools, just the same. And what makes
the situation even worse is that they have aided and abetted the
rise of "interest groups" that have no respect for the appropriate
roles of the executive, legislative, and judicial branches. The pres-

sure has been on the courts increasingly to assume legislative functions in competition with the legislature. As a result, the courts have grown to resemble the legislature. The courts are no longer a bastion of protection for property. In part, this is because the courts have permitted the concept of property to "evolve" to accommodate judges' new legislative functions. The concept of property as a fixed set of recognized uses is dead; property is now merely a right to due process. Judges seem satisfied if litigants "have their day in court." Gone too is the notion of property as a buffer between citizens and the state.

Many of the complaints against the civil justice system revolve around single issues or even single cases. But no amount of correction at these levels will cure the problem; to try to change the system piecemeal would be like building sand castles on the beach while the tide rolled in. Any meaningful reform has to look to the central question of property as the main bulwark for liberty. And any meaningful reform must be committed to restoring proper limits on judges *and* legislators. In an age when the state has transformed itself into a general moral agent and when government tends to a sort of "totalism," this will not be an easy project. Regaining respect for property will require rethinking our concept of the state and rediscovering the Framers' forgotten wisdom.

Notes

[1] Certainly there have been democracies with "mixed" forms of government combining politics and state control with market process and individual choice, but at the core of each democratic society is always the presently much-maligned institution of private property.

[2] "Elites" is admittedly a broad term; I am using it here to refer to individuals who: hold positions of influence in higher education, the media, and government; champion the "public good" over individual rights; and oppose the strong limits on government that the Framers had in mind when drafting the Constitution.

[3] To use an analogy, property is diagnosed as a cancer that starts small enough but soon destroys the body politic.

[4] Class is central to elites, and class is always either an abstraction based on speculation or an artifice, because it is based on some measure of social coercion.

[5]When the risk of violation primarily concerns conflict between individuals over the use of property, and when the consequences primarily affect only these individuals, we rely on a civil justice system. When the threat extends more broadly and puts the system at risk, criminal justice is employed.

[6]The landowners' only consolation was that they might benefit financially from an increase in trade once the roads were safer for commercial traffic.

[7]Whereas the old common law stressed personal responsibility and fixed outcomes, modern law and legislation stress flexibility and convenience. Legislation permits the law to respond quickly to innovation. It in particular provides for a quick fix based on a general observation. It also remains open to repeated quick-fix adjustments. The process, however, renders property contingent, problematic, and transitory.

GEORGE ROCHE

Capitalism and the Rule of the Law

Most people think of economics and the law as two distinct realms that intersect only on rare occasions. In truth, they intersect so often that they are practically inseparable. Our history provides ample testimony. Think, for example, of the late eighteenth century. What were the main causes of the American Revolution? Taxation without representation and growth of state regulation. After decades of hardship and struggle, the colonists who settled the eastern shores of North America finally achieved prosperity. Commerce and industry thrived. Meanwhile, in Great Britain, Parliament and the Crown were so caught up in their own affairs that they paid very little attention to what was happening thousands of miles away in the New World.

Largely by accident, then, the colonists enjoyed a remarkable, and unprecedented, degree of freedom. Historians refer to this as the period of "Salutary Neglect." But a new idea was gaining currency among the intellectual and political elite of Europe. It was called "mercantilism," and it held that the colonies existed solely to serve the interests of the Empire, and the interests of the state in particular. Thus, in the 1760s and 1770s, a series of restrictive regulations were imposed. The Proclamation of 1763 prohibited western expansion beyond the Appalachian Mountains. The old Navigation Acts dating back to the 1650s were "reinterpreted" to curb colonial commerce. The Stamp Act (1765) required taxes on all printed material, from newspapers and books to marriage licenses and deeds. The Declaratory Act (1766) made colonial legislatures subordinate to the king and Parliament. The Townshend

Acts (1767) levied duties on imports of basic goods like tea, ink, glass, and paper. The Quartering Act (1765) forced families to provide free lodging to British troops. This was not only taxation without representation but a blatant attack on the traditional rights of Englishmen—rights colonists had enjoyed for well over a century.

Economic Liberties and the Constitution

One member of the Virginia legislature, a planter by the name of George Washington, was so disturbed by these events that in April of 1769 he wrote a letter stating: "At a time when our lordly masters in Great Britain will be satisfied with nothing less than the deprivation of American freedom, it seems highly necessary that something should be done to avert the stroke and maintain the liberty which we have derived from our ancestors. . . ." He, like many of the most prominent leaders in the colonies, agreed to serve in the First Continental Congress in 1774. Fifty delegates from the thirteen colonies gathered together to debate how to respond to British oppression, but they failed to reach a consensus. The Second Continental Congress met in 1775, after the first shots between the Redcoats and the Minutemen were fired at Lexington and Concord. Washington attended this Congress in his old militia uniform, signaling that he thought the time to raise an army had come at last. John Adams, the Massachusetts delegate, nominated the "gentleman from Virginia" as commander-in-chief. His election was unanimous.

In July 1776, another Virginian, Thomas Jefferson, retired to the upstairs bedroom of a bricklayer's home in Philadelphia where he labored for eight days to produce a short statement now known as the Declaration of Independence. Think of the language of the Declaration:

> . . . He [George III] has forbidden his Governors to pass Laws of immediate and pressing importance. . . . He has dissolved Representative Houses repeatedly for opposing with manly firmness his invasions on the rights of the people. . . . He has made Judges dependent on his Will alone, for the tenure of their offices. . . . He has erected a multitude of New Offices,

and sent hither swarms of Officers to harass our people, and eat out their substance. . . . He has combined with others to subject us to a jurisdiction foreign to our constitution and unacknowledged by our laws . . . for cutting off our trade with all parts of the world:—for imposing taxes without our Consent. . . .

There is much more in the same vein, but what Jefferson was saying was that the colonists were willing to fight for their legal system and for economic liberties. They realized that it was only through the legal system—through the rule of law, rather than the rule of tyranny—that economic liberties would be protected.[1]

The American Revolution proved to be a tremendous military victory. A relatively small group of undisciplined, untrained, semiliterate farmers and tradesmen beat the world's greatest and most feared army. But it also proved to be something even more world-shaking: It was a revolution in understanding. For centuries, nations had operated on the premise that the state was the source of all legitimate power and that it granted rights to the people as its rulers saw fit. Suddenly, here was a totally new system in which it was acknowledged that "all Men are created equal, that they are endowed by their Creator with certain unalienable Rights, that among these are Life, Liberty, and the Pursuit of Happiness— That to secure these rights governments are instituted among Men, deriving their just Powers from the Consent of the Governed. . . ." Under such a system, the future of America looked bright indeed— for all of about one minute. Then reality set in.

After the Revolution, Congress was bankrupt. There was no treasury to pay off the enormous war debt, which was estimated at between sixty and eighty million dollars. There was no sound currency. There was no real unity between the fledgling states. As one historian points out, the United States at that time "was not one nation but thirteen." The Articles of Confederation—drafted in 1771 and finally ratified in 1781—was not strong enough to solve these serious economic problems. To make matters worse, in late 1786, a mob of poor farmers vainly tried to prevent tax foreclosures on their property by seizing a military arsenal filled with thousands of weapons. Known as Shay's Rebellion, this act shocked the nation and led Washington, former commander-in-chief of the Continental Army, to agree to preside over the controversial Constitutional Convention in Philadelphia in 1787. Washington had no love for tax collectors. In fact, he was deeply sympathetic toward the farmers' plight. But he could not condone lawlessness, no matter how great the provocation. He had risked his life during the Revolution; now, as president of the Constitutional Convention, he was risking his reputation for the meetings in Philadelphia were widely condemned as a secret plot to institute a monarchy or, at the very least, to rob the states of their authority. He realized, however, "that what was at issue was the grand question of whether a people could govern themselves by a reasonable process of deliberation rather than by the violent forces of arms to which every other government on earth owed its origins. In a sense, the Constitutional Convention would be legislating for all mankind."

In the end, Washington's gamble paid off: The convention was a success for it produced the U.S. Constitution, which was then ratified by the required number of states in 1788. In 1791, ten amendments known as the Bill of Rights were added. It is important to note that James Madison—the major intellectual force behind both the Constitution and the Bill of Rights—said that "every word . . . decides a question between power and liberty." And we should also note that the overwhelming number of these liberties to which Madison refers are economic liberties. Why is this so? I think it is because the founding fathers firmly believed in the ancient conception of justice that dated back to the time of the Greeks, Romans, and Hebrews. According to this conception, justice is both a *principle* and a *process* that protects not only a person's life but his property. It is also based on the idea that a man can only be truly free if he is the master of his destiny, and this means that he must be allowed to make his own decisions in the marketplace and reap the rewards of his own labor.

Among its many important legacies, the Constitution also established the following legal and economic principles:

1. that government must be frugal;
2. that government's powers to tax and spend should be strictly limited;
3. that massive debt is a threat to liberty;

4. that courts exist to protect private property and honor the sanctity of contracts;
5. that commerce and industry should be allowed to thrive; and
6. that every aspect of free enterprise—from buying and selling to accumulating wealth and investing it—should be allowed to flourish.

Modern Mercantilism

The Constitution established all these principles two centuries ago. Unfortunately, we have been less than faithful to them over the years. In the late nineteenth century, we began to listen to the siren call of Hegel and Marx, Old World philosophers who argued that only some form of socialism can ensure justice and prosperity. In the early to mid-twentieth century we were seduced by seemingly moderate and dispassionate economist experts like John Maynard Keynes who promoted the same thing under the guise of the "planned economy." What we have fallen for is essentially a modern mercantilism, which has allowed us to at least tolerate, if not eagerly embrace, big government, overregulation, price and production controls, central planning . . . in short, the very same offenses that caused our forefathers to revolt in the eighteenth century. But modern mercantilism is more than just a collection of statist programs and policies. It is a form of coercion that only begets more coercion. First, it centralizes power. This power disrupts the normal activity of the private sector. Then it justifies further centralization and disruption in order to solve the problems it created in the first place. Worse yet, it corrupts those who wield the centralizing power. No person can stoop to using coercion against others without allowing the corrupting influence of that power to work its corruption upon him. However, politically necessary such interventions may appear to the modern mercantilist, he must first of all make an *ethical* choice to violate the decision-making power and personal dignity of another individual. He must seize power just as forcefully and brazenly as any tyrant.

To paraphrase the arguments of Samuel Lubell, the author of a book written many years ago called *The Future of American Politics,* modern mercantilism has also politicized virtually all economic life. The wages of most workers are political wages, reflecting regulatory pressures rather than the laws of supply and demand. The prices producers receive are political prices since they are affected by the same pressures, especially if subsidies are involved. The savings investors hold are political savings, since their real value is determined by tax rates and investment laws. The end result of politicization is, of course, a power-oriented society that grows more and more monolithic since individual decisions and achievements are not of much consequence. The average person no longer looks to his own talents to get ahead; he looks to the state, since the state has the greatest power. In *Troilus and Cressida,* Shakespeare understood how this leads to the collapse of society. He wrote:

> Then everything includes itself in power;
> Power into will, will into appetite;
> And appetite, a universal wolfe,
> So doubly seconded with will and power,
> Must make perforce a universal prey,
> And last eat up himself.

Once natural law, decentralization, and freedom in the marketplace are no longer accepted as the bulwarks of the private sector, power, appetite, and will find every area of society a proper sphere for a further extension of coercive authority. Intervention is piled upon intervention, and power both encourages and feeds upon the strife between factions as they struggle to prosper through the intervention of power in their favor. As the exercise of power grows steadily greater and more damaging, antisocial tendencies and naked aggression increase. Meanwhile, the average person, already stripped of any higher dignity that does not emanate from the state, must make do with an illusory social welfare, the promise of better things to come, for his acquiescence in this new system.[2] For all ills are now to be solved by the passage of regulations and by coercive power. The individual cannot be held responsible for himself.

Surely, we are witnessing the rise of this new social being—the irresponsible individual—in America right now. Every troubling news story, statistic, and cultural index reveals that the irresponsibility is indeed reaching epidemic proportions. We see it in the moral breakdown of families, schools, neighborhoods, and the public square. We see it in the increasingly divisive debate over such issues as race, creed, and gender. We have become a nation of resentful victims and whining co-dependents, and we seem to have lost the fierce independence and resourcefulness of our forefathers.

The Responsible Individual

It may seem simplistic, but encouraging everyday personal responsibility is the key to restoring our strength as a nation and as a people. We should not forget about ideology, causes, public policy prescriptions, or political reform. These things *are* important. But they are not what we need to regard as first and foremost. This is because none of these things can be meaningful without the responsible individual. What has made America work, and work so well, is the fact that millions of average Joes get up in the morning and fulfill their daily obligations. Some of these obligations are quite ordinary: feeding the kids and helping them with homework after school; stopping at traffic lights and showing up at work on time; paying bills and honoring contracts. And some are extraordinary: risking one's life in defense of country; volunteering time and money for the welfare of others; and standing up for what is right, just, and true no matter what the cost.

We need to encourage more Americans to choose to be responsible. This is much tougher than it sounds, for we live in a culture that is increasingly self-absorbed and dependent on government. But I believe we can do it by restoring such vital and time-tested institutions as capitalism and the rule of law. These are institutions that make personal responsibility attractive and rewarding. Adam Smith was right when he observed that people respond to incentives. In the very same year in which Jefferson wrote the Declaration of Independence, this professor of moral philosophy at the University of Glasglow published a monumental study of human affairs called the *Wealth of Nations.* Concerned with the problems of free choice as a necessary foundation for an understanding of moral philosophy, Smith delved into the then-unknown field of political economy to discover what institutions promoted free choice. His work coincided with Jefferson's not only in time but in philosophy as well. Both the Declaration and *Wealth of Nations* summarized what the best thinkers of the late eighteenth century had come to realize: Individual freedom provides not only the means but the ends of a truly just society. This idea was courageously championed in open defiance of George III, the English king determined to remake the world in the image of mercantilism. Smith provided the economic blueprint for the outpouring of human energy, while Jefferson and the rest of the Founders provided the political framework of limited government within which a free economic system could operate.

In *Wealth of Nations*, a truly radical philosophy of wealth was espoused for the first time. To Adam Smith, wealth consisted of the goods consumed by *all* members of society. Kingly treasure, stores of bullion, state-granted monopolies, guilds—these old definitions of wealth were swept aside by a new system in which the production and consumption of all society was to be encouraged. It was a radical idea indeed. And America was the ideal place for it to flourish. Unlike Europe, hamstrung as it was by a long record of government interference, America was virgin territory where capitalism could establish itself from the very beginning. It was accepted on moral and legal grounds by the entire colonial society without reservation. This was the right way to do business, and the colonists knew it. Not even the mercantilist interference of politicians back in England could stop them. The colonists simply ignored the fantastic web of bounties, drawbacks, tariffs, rebates, regulations, and quotas that lay at the heart of the mercantilist system. In the words of journalist and author John Chamberlain:

> The North American colonies, too, had raised smuggling to a fine art. The colonists ignored the Molasses Acts, lured British coastguard ships into shoal waters where they grounded, and traded in and out of the Caribbean for rum and sugar quite as they pleased. The standard of life rose in North America every time a king's agent was bilked, a tax avoided. Wages were high in New York, money earned good interest,

yet the necessaries of life were cheap. Said Adam Smith in 1776: "The price of provisions is everywhere in North America much lower than in England. A dearth has never been known there." America was doing very well, thank you, without any Benevolent or Enlightened Despot's Five-Year Plan, and once the menace of the French had been removed by British and colonial successes in Canada during the French and Indian War, there seemed less reason than ever to put up with any nonsense that violated the immemorial rights of Englishmen on North American shores.

Smith's description of how this capitalist system works in operation was amazingly simple: Free individual self-interest to allow the members of society to pursue private gain and the result will be the production of the goods and services which society wants, in the quantities that society can use, and at the prices which society is prepared to pay. The first tenet of capitalism is, therefore, that self-interest makes the market work. Smith wrote in 1776, "It is not from the benevolence of the butcher, the brewer, or the baker that we expect our dinner, but from their regard to their self-interest. We address ourselves, not to their humanity, but to their self-love, and never talk to them of our necessities, but of their advantages." What keeps these selfish pursuers of self-interest from gouging society or from indulging in irresponsible behavior? The answer is the second tenet of capitalism: Competition. In a society free from political coercion, the only means of garnering the rewards that society offers is to compete effectively in meeting society's needs.[3]

Smith also argued that the law must maximize rather than limit the benefits of self-interest and competition by protecting private prosperity, eliminating trade barriers, and giving the buyers and sellers (of everything from goods and services to labor and capital) the freedom to determine their own terms of exchange. He, like the Founders, would never have suggested that he had the final answers. In fact, one of his basic premises was that no one ever has the final answers. The framework can be provided, the individual can be freed, but he must find his own "answers." That is what genuine freedom is all about.

Notes

[1] Elsewhere, I have made the argument that the assault on the colonists' religious liberties was also a major cause of the American Revolution. I do not mean to reject that argument; I am simply concentrating on the legal and economic factors in this essay.

[2] In a 1949 book, *On Power*, Bertrand de Jouvenel predicted the fate of a society in which power is centralized: "The social hierarchy is in ruins; the individual members are like peas shelled from their pods and form a numerical whole composed of equal elements. The state is the beginning and end of organization; it must apply itself to the task with the highest degree of authority and attention to detail. But is that to say that there are no longer any privileged persons? There are indeed; but as regards the state they are no longer privileged as men, preceding its authority. They hold their privileges in and from the state."

[3] In the 1770s, Adam Smith gave the world the first comprehensive analysis of individual economic choice, competition, and specialization. In the 1840s, the French economist Frederic Bastiat emphasized freedom in transactions as a further prerequisite of a properly functioning market. And in the 1870s, Austrian School of economics founder Carl Menger contributed the "subject theory of value," which held that a commodity is worth no more or less than the value it has to the prospective buyer. All three of these champions of freedom fully understood and appreciated the fact that truly creative action is voluntary action.

CLINT BOLICK

The Grassroots Legal Reform Movement

"Vincent Cummins looks out from his van with the hardened eyes of a criminal," writes John Tierney in the *New York Times Magazine.*[1] He describes the scene:

> [Cummins] looks left and right. No police cars in sight. None of the usual unmarked cars, either. Cummins pauses for a second—he has heard on the C.B. that cops have just busted two other drivers—but he can't stop himself. "Watch my back!" he repeats into the radio as he ruthlessly pulls over to the curb.
>
> Five seconds later, evil triumphs. *A middle-aged woman with a shopping bag climbs into the van . . . and Cummins drives off with impunity!* His new victim and the other passengers laugh when asked why they're riding this illegal jitney. What fool would pay $1.50 to stand on the bus or subway when you're guaranteed a seat here for $1? . . . "It takes me an hour to get home if I use the bus," explains Cynthia Peters, a nurse born in Trinidad. "When I'm working late, it's very scary waiting in the dark for the bus and then walking the three blocks home. With Vincent's van, I get home in less than half an hour. He takes me right to the door and waits until I get inside."

Adapted from "The Necessity of Judicial Action" in *Changing Course: Civil Rights at the Crossroads* (New Brunswick, NJ: Transaction Books, 1988).

That Vincent Cummins ever could be considered a criminal is a sobering sign of the confused times in which we live. To judge from the plethora of laws, regulations, and law enforcement resources devoted to it, one could infer that the most heinous crime in America is trying to earn an honest living. But, of course, the entrepreneurs do their best to persist, even if it means operating outside the law. As John Tierney puts it, "At this very moment, despite the best efforts of the police and the Transport Workers Union, somewhere in New York a serial predator like Cummins is luring another unsuspecting victim. He may even be making change for a $5 bill."[2]

One of the glaring obstacles to civil rights in America today is the pervasive regulation of economic opportunities by the government. These regulations frustrate—and in some cases prohibit outright—opportunities to participate and advance in the American economic system, even insofar as the ability to earn a basic living. Such restrictions are unequal in intent and effect, blatantly benefiting some, while burdening those who need such opportunities the most. A frontal assault against arbitrary governmental barriers to economic opportunities must occupy a primary thrust of the civil rights movement in the coming decades, and judicial action can provide a potent weapon.

That judicial action can be particularly well-suited to removing governmental barriers to economic opportunities is underscored by a line of Supreme Court precedents spanning several decades from the 1890s until the New Deal. During this era, the Supreme Court provided significant protection for economic liberty against arbitrary government actions, relying on the plain language of the Fourteenth Amendment, particularly its prohibition against state action that deprives individuals of liberty or property without due process of law.

The Golden Era of Economic Freedom

This philosophy was forcefully articulated by the four dissenters in the *Slaughter-House Cases* in 1873 who protested that the state-imposed slaughterhouse monopoly was invalid under the Fourteenth Amendment as a matter of civil rights. As Justice Field proclaimed, "That amendment was intended to give practical effect to the Declaration of 1776 of inalienable rights, rights which are the gift of the Creator, which the law does not confer, but only recognizes."[3] But upholding the state monopoly, Field argued, "the right of free labor, one of the most sacred and imprescriptable rights of man, is violated."[4] Likewise, Justice Bradley protested that "the individual citizen, as a necessity, must be left free to adopt such calling, profession, or trade as may seem to him most conducive. . . . Without this right he cannot be a freeman."[5]

It took until the following decade for the dissenters to prevail, but when they did it signaled the start of a golden era for economic freedom. The vital connection between civil rights and economic liberty was highlighted in *Yick Wo* v. *Hopkins,* one of the early decisions of this period. The case involved a San Francisco ordinance requiring approval by the Board of Supervisors to operate a laundry and mandating that all laundries be constructed of brick or stone. The ordinance was clearly aimed at Chinese entrepreneurs, whose laundries were predominantly housed in wooden structures. Under the ordinance, 150 Chinese were arrested for violations and 200 were denied permission to operate, despite the fact that many had been in business for twenty years or more and all had obtained certificates of safety under the prior standards. The Court invalidated the ordinance, characterizing it as "a naked and arbitrary power"[6] that rendered laundry operators "tenants at will, under the supervisors, of their means of living."[7] Although the law was "fair on its face and impartial in appearance," it was "administered by public authority with an evil eye and an unequal hand," thus violating the principle of equal protection of the laws.[8] The Court reaffirmed its commitment to the traditional civil rights vision in a profound proclamation of the nexus between economic liberty and individual freedom:

> [I]n our system, while sovereign powers are delegated to the agencies of government, sovereignty itself remains with the people, by whom and for whom all government exists and acts. . . . [T]he very idea that one may be compelled to hold his life, or the means of living, or any material right essential

to the enjoyment of life, at the mere will of another, seems to be intolerable in any country where freedom prevails, as being the essence of slavery itself.[9]

The highest expression of these principles—as well as a foreshadowing of their demise—came in *Lochner* v. *New York* in 1905. By a 5–4 majority, the Court struck down a New York statute setting maximum hours for bakery workers. Justice Peckham declared that whether the law "is or is not repugnant to the Constitution . . . must be determined from [its] natural effect . . . when put into operation, and not from [its] proclaimed purpose."[10] He reasoned "[t]he employee may desire to earn the extra money which would arise from his working for more than the prescribed time, but this statute forbids the employer from permitting the employee to earn it"; and since the "right to purchase or sell labor is part of the liberty" protected by the Fourteenth Amendment, the statute was plainly unconstitutional.[11] Noting that adequate health and safety standards already existed to protect bakery workers,[12] Justice Peckham assailed the paternalism implicitly in the statute:

> There is no contention that bakers as a class are not equal in intelligence and capacity to men in other trades or manual occupations, or that they are not able to assert their rights and care for themselves without the protecting arm of the state interfering with their independence of judgment and action. They are in no sense wards of the state.[13]

Thus did the majority in *Lochner* proclaim the right of the individual to determine his or her own destiny—the essence of civil rights.

The Decline of Economic Freedom

But the dissent by Justice Holmes[14] provided the reactionary rationale for judicial abdication in the area of economic liberty that would finally prevail several decades later and that dominates the conventional jurisprudential wisdom even today. Holmes charged that "[t]his case is decided upon an economic theory which a large part of this country does not entertain," namely, the "shibboleth" of "[t]he liberty of the citizen to do as he likes so long as he does not interfere with the liberty of others to do the same."[15] On the contrary, Holmes contended, "a constitution is not intended to embody a particular economic theory."[16] Instead, Holmes preferred a "reasonableness" standard,[17] under which almost any invasion of economic liberty—even if it is "injudicious" or "tyrannical"[18]—would be sanctioned.

The ramifications of Holmes' dissent were disastrous. Solicitor General Charles Fried perceptively observes that "Holmes' argument summarizes the source of our modern intellectual difficulties when it contends that the Constitution was not intended to embody a particular economic theory." That "may be true of other constitutions," Fried explains, "but it's not true of ours, which was organized upon very explicit principles of political theory."[19]

The Supreme Court continued to protect economic liberty until the New Deal, during which the Roosevelt appointees ultimately tipped the balance in favor of providing carte blanche authority to governmental entities to control economic activities and stifle entrepreneurial opportunities. By 1955, the metamorphosis was complete. In *Williamson* v. *Lee Optical*, the Court sustained a statute prohibiting opticians from duplicating old or broken eyeglass lenses and from fitting old lenses into new frames without a prescription from a licensed physician. Justice Douglas, writing for the Court, failed to comprehend the connection between civil rights and economic liberty. Even though the "law may exact a needless, wasteful requirement," Douglas ruled, "it is for the legislature, not the courts, to balance the advantages and disadvantages of the new requirement."[20] Douglas pronounced the death knell of one of the proudest chapters of American jurisprudence, declaring "[t]he day is gone when this Court uses the . . . Fourteenth Amendment to strike down state laws . . . because they may be unwise, improvident, or out of harmony with a particular school of thought.[21] Unfortunately, the "school of thought" so casually dismissed by the Court is the very natural rights philosophy upon which the Constitution—as well as the American civil rights vision—is based.

A more recent case illustrates how utterly the Court has abandoned economic liberty, and how dire are the consequences flowing from its abdication. In the 1976 case of *City of New Orleans* v. *Dukes*, the Court was presented with a classic, arbitrary licensing restriction that erected a barrier to the quintessential entry-level entrepreneurial enterprise—hot dog pushcarts. The plaintiff, Dukes, had operated her pushcart in the French Quarter for several years until a New Orleans ordinance was passed to prohibit such food sales, thus depriving Dukes of her livelihood. But, as most licensing statutes do, the ordinance provided a "grandfather clause," for long-term operators, of which there were only two. The courts of appeals struck the ordinance under the Fourteenth Amendment as totally arbitrary and irrational, but the Supreme Court sustained the law, declaring that under the Amendment, "this Court consistently defers to legislative determinations as to the desirability of particular statutory discriminations."[22] At least insofar as the Fourteenth Amendment was concerned, the Court made it clear the state was free to destroy economic freedom with impunity.

The Current Situation

Today, no member of the Supreme Court appears willing to revive the *Lochner* doctrine. In fact, many conservatives condemn any such effort. They argue that during the *Lochner* era, the judiciary improperly substituted its will for that of the legislature. But the crucial point they miss is that the Court did so only when the legislature impermissibly substituted *its* will for the fundamental rights of individuals. Any conservative should agree with the proposition, stated by Justice Sutherland in 1932, that "in our constitutional system . . . there are certain essentials of liberty with which the state may not dispense."[23] If this is true—if our Constitution is not a blanket grant of power to government, but a limitation of its powers, as the Framers understood it—then the judiciary must play a central role in safeguarding the precious fundamental liberties we call "civil rights."

We have lost a great deal of ground since *Lochner*, and a creative and principled litigation strategy to restore judicial protection for economic liberty is critically important. But unfortunately, it is simply not presently feasible to premise such a strategy upon an explicit revival of *Lochner*, given the disdain with which that doctrine is viewed by most jurists, both liberal and conservative. Instead, the civil rights movement must rely upon mainstream litigation vehicles while consistently emphasizing the vital nexus between civil rights and economic liberty.

Some evidence exists that the judiciary may be sympathetic to a modified *Lochner* approach. While some commentators believe that substantive rights have been read out of the Fourteenth Amendment altogether, the Supreme Court has recently suggested there are some limits to the deference it is willing to accord to state regulations. Specifically, for the first time since *Lochner*, the Court is looking behind regulations to determine whether they are actually "rational" or "reasonable," rather than simply presuming their validity.[24] Accordingly, the civil rights movement should aggressively challenge barriers to entry and equal participation in the marketplace as violations of equal protection under the Fourteenth Amendment, in tandem with 42 U.S.C. § 1983, which provides a right to sue state or local governments for deprivations of rights "under color of state law."[25]

To the extent such obstacles create disproportionate burdens upon minorities, it may be possible to invoke "strict scrutiny," which typically results in invalidation of the state action. This possibility is limited by the Supreme Court's admonition that constitutional attacks against state action under the Fourteenth Amendment require proof of intent to discriminate on the basis of race, which is often difficult or impossible to prove.[26] Nonetheless, many contemporary economic restraints, such as licensing laws, trace their roots to blatantly racist antecedents in the Jim Crow era. At the heart of every barrier to entry lurks an intent to exclude *someone*—itself a violation of the principle of equal protection of the laws—and in many cases that inherently evil motive may be sufficiently tinged with racism to invoke heightened judicial scrutiny.

Light on the Horizon

Progress on restoring economic liberty as a fundamental civil right is slow but steady. Since launching the Institute for Justice in 1991, my colleagues and I have trained our litigation arsenal on regulatory barriers that prevent hardworking people from earning an honest living. Some successes—such as ending Denver's taxicab monopoly—came mainly through the court of public opinion. Others have occurred in the courtroom, providing building blocks for future cases—and the foundation from which to eventually call upon the Supreme Court to overturn the *Slaughter-House Cases.*

The first victory came in 1989, when a federal district court in Washington D.C. overturned a Jim Crow-era ban on streetcorner shoeshine stands.[27] A few years later, a federal judge struck down the Houston Anti-Jitney Law of 1924, which was passed at the behest of the streetcar industry to squelch competition from jitneys (or today, commuter vans). "The purpose of the statute was economic protectionism in its most glaring form, and this goal is not legitimate," the Court declared. "The ordinance has long-outlived its ill-begotten existence."[28] Most recently, a federal court in San Diego refused to dismiss an economic liberty challenge to California cosmetology licensing laws on behalf of American hair-braiders.[29]

Already, new cases are underway to vindicate economic liberty —including a lawsuit challenging New York City's ban on commuter vans on behalf of Vincent Cummins and other entrepreneurs. The spectacle of welfare recipients having a greater "right" to receive their public assistance than entrepreneurs have to pursue an honest living is a blight on a national doctrinally committed to economic freedom. We should make a top priority of restoring the essential economic liberty that is every American's birthright— every American's *civil* right.

Notes

[1]John Tierney, "Man with a Van," *New York Times Magazine* (August 10, 1997).
[2]Tierney, "Man with a Van."
[3]*Slaughter-House Cases*, 83 U.S. 36, 105 (1873) (Field, J., dissenting).
[4]Ibid., 110.
[5]Ibid., 116 (Bradley, J., dissenting).
[6]*Yick Wo* v. *Hopkins*, 118 U.S. 356, 366 (1886).
[7]Ibid., 368.

[8]Ibid., 373–74.

[9]Ibid., 370.

[10]*Lochner* v. *New York,* 198 U.S. 45, 64 (1905).

[11]Ibid., 52–53.

[12]Ibid., 61–62.

[13]Ibid., 57.

[14]Justice Holmes is revered by many as a great jurist, but the reasons for such historical stature escape this author. His opinions, like his dissent in *Lochner,* reveal a remarkably authoritarian tendency. See, e.g., *Davis* v. *Massachusetts,* 167 U.S. 43 (1897), affirming the conviction of a preacher for making a speech in the Boston Common without a permit; *Patterson* v. *Colorado,* 205 U.S. 454 (1907), upholding the conviction of a cartoonist for satirizing the Colorado Supreme Court; and *Block* v. *Hirsh,* 256 U.S. 134 (1921), sustaining the suspension of private property rights of landlords during World War I.

[15]*Lochner,* 75 (Holmes, J., dissenting).

[16]Ibid., 76.

[17]Ibid., 77.

[18]Ibid., 75.

[19]"Crisis in the Courts," *Manhattan Report on Economic Policy,* Vol. 5, No. 2 (1982), 4.

[20]*Williamson* v. *Lee Optical,* 348 U.S. 483, 487 (1955).

[21]Ibid., 488.

[22]*City of New Orleans* v. *Dukes,* 427 U.S. 297, 303 (1976).

[23]*New State Ice Co.* v. *Liebmann,* 285 U.S. 262 (1932).

[24]For a discussion of these cases and their potential significance, see David O. Stewart, "A growing equal protection clause?" *ABA Journal* (October 1985), 108–20. Unlike many of the cases decided in the *Lochner* era, which were decided under the "liberty" clause of the Fourteenth Amendment, these case—*City of Cleburne* v. *Cleburne Living Center,* 105 S. Ct. 3249 (1985); *Metropolitan Life Insurance Co* v. *Ward,* 105 S. Ct. 1676 (1985); and *Williams* v. *Vermont,* 105 S. Ct. 2465 (1985)—were decided under the equal protection clause.

[25]*Monnell* v. *Department of Soial Services,* 436 U.S. 658 (1978).

[26]*Washington* v. *Davis,* 426, U.S. 229, 239–40 (1976).

[27]*Brown* v. *Barry,* 710 F. Supp. 352 (D.D.C. 1989).

[28]*Santos* v. *City of Houston,* 852 F. Supp. 601 (S.D. Tex. 1994).

[29]*Cornwell* v. *California Board of Barbering and Cosmetology,* 962 F. Supp. 1260 (S.D. Cal. 1997).

WILLIAM S. MORRIS, III

Capitalism, the Law, and the Media Watchdog in American Society

I am a firm believer in our free marketplace, where buyer and seller can meet with minimum government interference or regulation.

And I certainly believe in the rule of law: to protect each citizen's rights and to ensure honest, safe, and orderly conduct of the nation's affairs, both public and private.

But I submit that a "free society" rests not just on the two pillars of capitalism and the rule of law but also on an equally important third pillar—free speech. Without it, the first two pillars would tumble.

Our forefathers knew this. They reaffirmed the right to free speech in the first amendment to the Constitution. If there were no free speech, it would be impossible to run our system of checks and balances, through which we are able to maintain the liberty that allows the free market to flourish.

The Media's Dual Personality

Every day, we in the media wrestle with issues of personal and corporate self-interest versus serving the public good. We agonize over questions of meeting the public's need to know versus protecting the individual's right to privacy. We are often torn between our personal respect for the institutional pillars of our society—government, the law, business—and the historic role of the media as critics of those same institutions.

Every day, every newspaper of significance in this country struggles for success in a highly competitive free market—just like any other business. Whether privately or publicly owned, these newspapers must respond to shareholder demands for appropriate profits and return on investments—just like any other business. And, just like any other business, newspapers must operate under the umbrella of an orderly marketplace and the even-handed rule of law.

The media is in an interesting position, then, with its dual responsibilities, dual personalities. On one hand, it must uphold the noble and necessary rights of free speech as ordained by the Constitution of the United States. On the other, to survive, it must engage in the rough and tumble world of commerce, trying to make a go of it as a private industry.

Advocate or Foe?

Without a free press, nothing else in a free society would work.

So, why then are the media so often perceived as being at odds with society? Why are we so often depicted as foes of the business community, government, the law?

If we are part and parcel of the system, why are we so often perceived as attacking it?

More to the point, why is there a gap—call it a credibility gap, call it simple lack of trust—between journalists and business executives, lawyers, politicians, government officials, and even the very public we think we serve?

As you may imagine, we in the press have given this much thought and have developed a few ideas.

First, the power of newspapers to influence public opinion and policy—and the potential for misuse of that power—can be frightening. The media are not alone in this. All institutions of power in our society—government, business, labor unions, the law, even organized religion—take their knocks these days. Public distrust is running high, and no institution with power will escape it.

Second, critics of the press know—and we know—that we don't always use our power responsibly. We make mistakes. We can be arrogant. But the sins of our past are etched in modern journalism's collective memory. We know, we discuss, we study, and we labor to avoid betrayal of the public trust.

Third, the press sometimes is unfairly targeted by those who seek scapegoats for their own shortcomings. You know what I mean:

— The lawyer who blames his lost case on pretrial publicity, not his mistakes in the courtroom.
— The airline executive who blames his company's failing business on press coverage of the airplane crash, rather than on the crash itself.
— The politician who blames his policy's failure on press criticisms, not the basic weakness of the policy.
— The soldier who blames correspondent coverage for failure at war.
— The football coach who blames sports journalists for failure on the gridiron.
— The parent who blames the media for negatively influencing his wayward children.

The list is endless and, frankly, at times ridiculous.

There is another reason for the perception that we in the press somehow stand apart from the system and that we are insensitive or overly critical. This fourth reason, I firmly believe, is a basic misunderstanding of the role of the press in America and an underappreciation of the importance of the First Amendment.

Let me illustrate this point. As I explain my understanding of what the press is and what it must do, consider your understanding of our role. Then let's compare our understandings and see if there is a credibility gap.

We think the First Amendment is the core of American freedom, and we think the press is the first line in its defense. How would you vote if asked whether a communist should have free speech rights in America? Or a member of the Ku Klux Klan?

We think it is your First Amendment, and be you an Eagle Scout and all-round nice person or a rascal and a scoundrel, we will defend your right to speak your mind. How would you vote on whether a pornographer has the right to publish a magazine? Would you agree with us that to deny his right to publish is to deny your right—our right—to publish?

We in the press—as your surrogate—spend a great deal of time and money blasting open the cloakrooms of Congress, pushing open the doors of the local board of education, and exposing the otherwise secret conduct of public business to open scrutiny. Show me another industry that so effectively and tirelessly pushes, prods, and insists that you, the citizen, must have constant oversight of how your public affairs are conducted. Do you think reporters are "too pushy?" Too aggressive? Only out to get a good story? Only out to sell more newspapers, more magazines, more commercial minutes? Perhaps a few are, but the majority are committed to truth and fair-dealing.

Watching the Watchdog

Since colonial days, we in the press have seen ourselves as watchdogs over public affairs. We sound the alarm in the night when everyone else is sleeping soundly, blissfully unaware that wrongdoing is afoot. But sometimes you awaken and throw the shoe at *us*—to silence the noise, not to right the wrongdoing—and then you roll over, back to sleep.

We are the Fourth Estate, equal in responsibility to the other "estates"—the judicial, the executive, and the legislative branches of government. We see our power as a counterbalance to their potential misuse of their power.

But, who watches the watchdog?

That is a fair question, and I want to deal with it by asking you to do six things.

First, join the thoughtful, discerning Americans who have a sense of history and who resist those social commentators who clamor for government intervention in the journalistic process. Don't cave in to those who demand government regulation of the press. As refugees from totalitarianism, our Founding Fathers stood for a free press independent of—and watchful and critical of—government. If we are silenced, who will stand guard?

Second, let free market forces and the constitutional rule of law regulate the press. Editors know that if they don't serve your needs, you won't buy their newspapers. If our advertising pages don't create the proper marketplace for buyer and seller, advertisers will take their dollars elsewhere. Could any government regulator, could any bureaucrat, could any law provide a more effective discipline than marketplace discipline?

Third, understand that a free press will make mistakes, even perhaps abuse its power. We write the first, hurried, and sometimes ragged draft of history. Mistakes are inevitable, and our Founding Fathers understood this. A principal architect of our freedom, James Madison, decided that the greater good which results from a free press was worth the trade-off of having to accept some of the less salutory aspects. He wrote:

> It is better to leave a few of its noxious branches to their luxuriant growth, than, by pruning them away, to insure the vigour of those yielding the proper fruits.

Did Madison say that we must permit mistakes and abuse? Why?

To the press alone, chequered as it is with abuses, the world is indebted for all the triumphs which have been gained by reason and humanity over error and oppression.

Fourth, don't lump those supermarket tabloids together with the *Wall Street Journal*, the *New York Times*, and other mainstream newspapers. Be very careful to distinguish between television, which is obsessed with entertainment, and print journalism, which tries to inform.

Fifth, don't confuse the message and messenger. We report a lot of bad news these days, but remember: We don't start the wars, cause the floods and famines, or commit the crimes: We just report them.

And, sixth, remember that but for a free press things might not have turned out so well for this wonderful country of ours. For starters, we likely would not have achieved our independence from Britain.

Think of what the American public would not have known had they not had a free press:

— General MacArthur didn't tell us that he wanted to take us into war with China. But a free press did.
— The Pentagon didn't tell us that the Vietnam War was going badly. But a free press did.

— The White House didn't tell us about Watergate or White-
water. But a free press did.

Without an unfettered flow of information, we cannot make
informed judgments about the character of the men and women
who presume to govern us. Without reporting on what is happening in our courtrooms, we cannot make informed decisions about
how our laws are made, interpreted, and enforced. Without analysis of economic trends or business ethics, we cannot improve our
job prospects, create new goods and services, or protect our free
enterprise system.Without access to the facts, and different perspectives on them, our only source of information would be the
skilled, well-financed, professional spinmeisters who offer only a
partial—and very sanitized—view.

So, argue with us, disagree; we'll even give you space in our
letters columns. But read us, listen to us, watch us, and make your
own judgments based on the facts.

BETTINA BIEN GREAVES

Ludwig von Mises
and Economic Law

It was in the fall of 1948 that Ludwig von Mises's seminar in economic theory began at New York University. I starting attending the seminars three years later, in the fall of 1951, and did regularly for eighteen years until Mises retired at age 89 in the spring of 1969.

Most people think it would be boring to take the same courses with the same professor year after year. But Mises never gave the same course twice: Each semester he addressed a different theme. The fall term might be devoted to epistemology, the spring term to monetary theory; the next fall he might discuss monopoly, and in the spring, bureaucracy. And he usually tried to keep discussions on track, turning aside questions that he considered irrelevant to the semester's theme. Here are a few of the topics, in no particular order, that he covered in the course of my eighteen years: entrepreneurship, competition, economic calculation, intervention, interest theory, praxeology, profits/losses, prices, inflation, epistemology, economic history, "macroeconomics," Marxism, positivism, institutionalism, and so on. Out of his in-depth approach, the serious student derived a thorough understanding of economics.

The Law of Human Action

One evening, Mises asked us seminar students what we thought an economic law was. All of a sudden I realized that there was really only *one* economic law, the law of action. The basis of all economics—from production, to prices, to consumption—is action, the action of individuals. That is why Mises titled his major economics book *Human Action.* Once you realize that all economic activities stem from what individuals do, you have the key to understanding all market operations, from the most simple to the most complex, from barter to money, from interpersonal trade to trade cycles. And from the law of action all other economic laws are derived—the laws of price, exchange, interest, supply and demand.

An understanding of the law of human action also provides an insight into history. Mises's lectures were rich in references to historical persons and events. He had always been intellectually curious, a prodigious reader, and over the years he acquired a wealth of historical knowledge. His interpretations of historical events did more than describe, they actually explained. Take, for example, the Industrial Revolution.

The Industrial Revolution of the eighteenth and nineteenth centuries is typically portrayed as a period of widespread poverty, exploitation, and misery. Men, women, and children were forced, it was held, by unscrupulous employers to work long hours under dangerous conditions and to live in dirty, crowded tenements. But Mises offered another interpretation.

In the first place, the Industrial Revolution was not strictly speaking a "revolution." The word "revolution" comes from the physical sciences and refers to the rotation of any object around a center or axis. The Industrial Revolution was not *that* kind of a revolution. The dictionary also defines a "revolution" as a total, sudden, or radical change in ideas or political organization. But, as Mises described the Industrial Revolution, it was not *that* kind of a "revolution" either. So what kind of a "revolution" was it?

The Industrial Revolution, as Mises saw it, was the consequence of the actions of countless individuals, a step-by-step development that came about as a consequence of a shift in ideas over many decades. The grounds for the Industrial Revolution were laid by an idea that first took hold in England—thanks to the work of such thinkers as Montesquieu, John Locke, David Hume, and Adam Smith—the idea that the power of the king and his lords should be limited and that individuals had rights which should be respected and protected.

The so-called Industrial Revolution may have started with nothing more momentous than the efforts of some small peddler who trudged the countryside with a pack of wool on his back. He would stop at tiny hovels where families were living and struggling to survive, drop off small batches of wool to be spun into yarn, then call back some days later to collect the yarn, pay the spinners a pittance for their efforts, and take the yarn to loom operators who wove it into cloth. Again and again the peddler would return. What he paid the farmer's family often made the difference between their eating or starving.

Liberated from the rigidities of the old feudal system, freed from the restrictions imposed by the king and his agents, people could begin to work and to think for themselves. A number of ingenious persons, no longer hampered by long-standing feudalistic rules and regulations, took advantage of the situation to find new ways of doing things and to produce new tools and machines. To name a few: James Watt developed the steam engine; James Hargreaves invented a multispindled spinning jenny to spin wool and cotton into yarn; Edmund Cartwright produced a power loom; and Richard Arkwright, a clever entrepreneur, helped to bring these several inventions together in factories.

The transition was gradual and sometimes painful. The factory system developed slowly from small beginnings. Some enterprising individual conceived the idea of bringing many spinners together under one roof. Instead of taking the wool to the spinners, the spinners came to the wool. One by one, factories were built alongside England's many rivers and streams, each powered by water wheels and housing some of the newly invented spinning jennies and weaving looms. People went to work in these factories because they wanted the money; they preferred working there to almost starving in their tiny huts out in the country.

During this period, new parts of the world were opening up to settlers. Some enterprising individuals tried exporting a few sheep to New Zealand and Australia, hoping they would flourish in those temperate climes. And they did. In time a new industry was created producing Australian and New Zealand wool to feed the new British factories.

Landowners, who no longer had to comply with feudal restrictions, experimented with new agricultural methods by irrigating, rotating crops, and fertilizing. They expanded their operations and, in the process, increased food production.

The Industrial Revolution that transformed feudal society into a society in which former serfs and tenant farmers had to find work on their own was long and often painful. However, in time food became more plentiful. More babies survived childhood. People began to live longer. Textiles soon were mass-produced inexpensively enough so that the members of poor families did not always have to wear hand-me-down rags, but could afford to buy new cloth now and then to make clothes for themselves. Over the years, thousands who had lived close to starvation, in virtual servitude with no opportunity of getting ahead, found better lives.

By describing the Industrial Revolution in this way, as the consequence of the ideas, actions, and choices of individuals, Mises explained not only the origins of the factory system but also showed how the Industrial Revolution itself brought about some of the most important changes in history, making it possible for more food, goods, and services, to be produced, thus enabling people to live longer, healthier lives.

Subjective Values and Prices

The theory of subjective value is at the core of Austrian economic theory, the theory for which Mises was a lifelong exponent. Every individual has his or her own personal (subjective) values, wants, aims, and goals, and these values guide every action. Just as all market activities may be traced to the actions of specific individuals, as in the Industrial Revolution, so may all their choices and decisions be traced to their personal (subjective) values, wants, aims, and goals.

In the field of economics, market values and market prices are determined by the values of the individuals involved. Every individual is always pursuing his or her own interests, striving for what he or she wants most. Individuals meet, personally and figuratively, on the market; they communicate, cooperate, trade, bid, compete, and deal with one another. Their eagerness, as they strive for what they want, reflects their personal values and is revealed by the amount they bid. The more effort and energy a person exerts in striving for something, the more that person is willing to offer. What an individual gives in terms of work, time, effort, or money for something is the "price" he or she pays. As many persons meet and compete with one another, ratios develop between the value individuals place on what they are offering and the value they place on what they are bidding for. These ratios reflect the personal values of the many bidders and offerers on the market and are known as "prices."

Although usually expressed in terms of money, prices as such are not simply quantities of money. They are something very different. Prices are ratios between what would-be sellers are asking and what would-be buyers are offering at a particular time and place. These ratios are determined by the interplay of individuals meeting on the market and they vary from time to time and from place to place. A specific ratio or "price" always reflects the personal values of the individuals appearing on the market at the time. Because prices are value-determined ratios that arise out of the actions and choices of market participants, it is not "prices" as such that government may decree or fix, but rather fiat-decreed quantities of money. Mises was thinking of prices as value-determined ratios when he wrote in his major economic treatise, *Human Action*: "A government can no more determine prices than a goose can lay hen eggs."

Everyone's values, priorities, and goals are always changing. Therefore, the "price" would-be buyers are willing to offer for any particular good or service and the "price" would-be sellers are willing to accept for that good or service changes as conditions change. Consider the price printed on a packaged loaf of bread in a grocery store. Or the price asked for a ton of steel at the foundry. These are not actual "prices"; they are merely *asking prices*. The bread or steel will trade at that money–goods ratio only if there is a taker. After an exchange has been completed that ratio may no longer prevail; a new potential buyer may refuse to pay that same "price." Or that potential buyer may be willing to offer even more to beat out competitors.

Prices are ratios agreed upon by would-be buyers and would-be sellers at a particular time and place. At other times and places, the prices agreed upon will reflect the personal values of other would-be buyers and would-be sellers and may be very different. Mises once compared the ephemeral nature of prices to snowflakes. Like a snowflake, every price is unique. It emerges only at the moment of exchange; then, once the exchange is completed, it vanishes.

Government Intervention

Mises did not just observe human action in the marketplace, he analyzed how the free choices of individuals were affected and distorted by government intervention. Mises' main job throughout his life in Vienna was with a government agency, the Austrian Chamber of Commerce. As its economic adviser, his responsibility was to advise the members of the Austrian Parliament and to comment on economic legislation. He also taught at the University of Vienna as a *Privatdozent,* a private nonsalaried lecturer; his pay came not from the university but from those who attended his lectures. Mises never became a full professor; the climate of opinion in Austria was against him. He was Jewish in a country that was increasingly anti-Semitic. He opposed government intervention in a country that was increasingly socialist. And he was uncompromising, refusing to endorse even minor restrictions on business and individual rights.

Perhaps Mises' uncompromising stand against government intervention was the biggest obstacle to his obtaining a full professorship. His refusal to compromise on this issue stemmed from his fervent wish to keep people from destroying civilization. Through his understanding of the subjective theory of value, he realized that the path to peace and prosperity rested on the protection of the rights of individuals. People should be free to deal with one another, to communicate, cooperate, and exchange voluntarily. Only free men operating in a society unhampered by outside interferences can prosper and live at peace with one another. Let's explain.

The theory of subjective value tells us that when two persons trade goods, services, and/or money voluntarily with one another, both parties expect to gain. Both are offering something they have for something they value still more. If not, they wouldn't bother to trade. If the anticipations of both parties prove correct, and no force or fraud is committed, both parties gain precisely because they have obtained something they valued more than what they relinquished. Both will be better off, more satisfied. From this it follows that when persons are free to strive for what they want, so long as they do not interfere with the equal rights of others, and when they are not hampered by force or fraud, they will improve their respective situations step-by-step. Thus, the tendency in a society that protects the rights and property of individuals and does not impinge on their freedom is for conditions to improve, for everyone to be better off.

Mises' understanding of the importance of the theory of subjective value for economics made him not only a determined foe of government intervention but also of inflation, which, with its close cousin "credit expansion," he considered the most insidious and dangerous of government interventions. Their cause seemed mysterious and hidden from most people, giving politicians an almost free hand to spend newly created money as they wished. But explaining how this happens and its consequences would take us pretty far afield.

In closing, therefore, I should like to give a few quotes to show how Mises illustrated economic theory in his lectures. In his books, he often used rather complex and difficult words because he wanted to be very precise. However, in speaking he often expressed himself quite colorfully. Here are a few samples:

> *On stockpiling:* "Governments frequently buy and store surplus goods like wheat and butter in the same way a wine merchant buys and stores wine. While wines improve with age, the same cannot be said of wheat and butter."

> *On big business:* "Many problems in the world have been blamed on big business, cartels, and trusts. But look at wine. Beginning with the Persian poet Omar Khayyám, author of the *Rubaiyat*, wine has been advertised by the poets. Were the poets then in the pay of the Whiskey Trust? Why not say that the desire for cleanliness is due to the Soap Trust?"

> *On prices:* "You say the secret is in selling something above cost. But the situation is really very different. The problem is to produce something for which consumers are willing to pay above cost."

On education: "Education can only hand down what was present in the old generation. The innovator cannot be educated. There is no school for the inventor."

On nationality and trade: "St. Francis of Assisi and Casanova were both Italians and they both spoke Italian. But they used that language for very different purposes."

On minimum wage laws: "Why should the members of Congress be so nasty as to fix a minimum wage below their own?"

On NASA's Apollo 11 mission in 1969: "It is very difficult to get away from the government. Now we can't even get away from the government on the moon."

On taxes: "Perhaps orangutans *could* talk if they wanted to, but they don't want to because they don't want to pay taxes."

On supply, demand, and production: After lecturing in San Francisco, Mises was being driven around the city. Their driver left the throughway and drove onto a city street lined with bars, restaurants, and night clubs. Mrs. Mises called the professor's attention to the signs: "Topless Bar," "Bottomless Bar," "Stark Naked Girls." Mises commented, "Very bad for the clothing industry."

On statistics: "Statistical averages conceal the truly significant factors. If a man has one leg on an iceberg and the other in a fire, the *average* is then all right."

On morality: "The real 'jewels' are morals."

Robert Formaini

Laissez-Faire:
Let Each Individual Choose

It is extraordinarily that I—an American citizen, living in the United States—feel that I must defend the proposition that individuals ought to be allowed to choose what they think is in their best interest. I say extraordinary because we live in a culture that, at first glance, seems to worship the concept of choice. Indeed, the appeal of the words "freedom of choice" is so politically powerful that the concept is often appropriated, disingenuously, by those whose true desire is clearly not the advancement of individual liberty. In fact, virtually every law acts to restrict the latitude of individual freedom in favor of extending the latitude of state activities. Since state activity is collective, the trend in America over the past two centuries is clear: an ever-shrinking scope for personal choice and freedom of action against an ever-widening set of state (collective) actions.

Consider this passage from Robert Nisbet's wonderful 1988 book, *The Present Age*:

> Any returned Framers of the Constitution would be quite as shocked by the extent and depth of the power of the national state in American lives today as they would be by war and the gargantuan military. [T]here can be no doubt of what the framers did not want: a highly centralized, unitary political Leviathan. That, however, is what their work of art has become in two centuries. And with this has come, has had to come, a political absolutism over Americans that would not be

lessened or mitigated for the Framers by its manifestly, unchallengeably democratic foundations.

What accounts for this remarkable transformation? Have we, as Americans, lost sight of the philosophical reasons for the founding of this nation? Or is it that the majority of us no longer support those foundations? It is an undeniable fact that we have moved, to use the words of the British historian A. J. P. Taylor, from a nation where a citizen's contact with the state amounted to greeting the post office delivery person, to the current reality where, every day and in virtually every human endeavor, we are constrained, cajoled, and often downright forced to act, speak, or choose in ways that are demanded by some level of government.

I recall quite vividly an argument I had with a fellow draftee as we were wasting part of our lives at Fort Gordon, Georgia, in 1970. (You see, I would not have chosen to spend those two years in the Army, but I was not allowed to make that choice—except by forfeiting my freedom or by leaving my native country altogether.) As I argued essentially the same case against state interventions as I have given above, he interrupted me to announce that all those laws that I was complaining about had given people *more freedom*, and that Americans were *freer* than they had ever been! This is a fairly common attitude in this country, and the fact that it is widely believed is testament not only to the power of reformist political myth, but to state interventions in every layer of our educational system, from daycare through doctoral study.

Most of us have heard about or read former President Eisenhower's parting words, warning us against what he called "the military-industrial complex." But how many of us remember his warnings about the relationship between the state and education, especially higher education, offered in that same Farewell Address?

> The prospect of domination of a nation's scholars by federal employment, project allocations, and the power of money is ever present—and gravely to be retarded. [P]artly because of the huge costs involved, a government contract becomes virtually a substitute for intellectual curiosity.

These words, written in 1960, represent a brilliant analysis of where higher education has ultimately gone—and why. Clearly Eisenhower's hope that this process be "gravely retarded" has not been realized. American education has sold out completely to the state at every level. The National Education Association is a completely ideologized, government-worshipping union that supports every move away from individualism and real education. Most of America's teachers and administrators react to the word "choice" like vampires react to crosses!

No one accuses state-run educational systems of promoting too much individualism and freedom of choice, except when referring to a very narrow set of "choices" that today are termed politically correct. But "politically correct choices" are not choices at all, but intellectual fashions held by a vocal and politically backed minority, and enforced at the point of a gun. The noble and essential concept of choice has been perverted in our time to a political slogan that mandates particular outcomes by law. Any one of you who believes that the reportage of the effects of government-backed (and often taxpayer-financed) political correctness is exaggerated need only read about Stanford University in David Sacks and Peter Thiel's excellent—and positively horrifying—book, *The Diversity Myth*. And while you read it, keep in mind the fact that Stanford is, according to current terminological usage, a "private" university.

Let's examine the fundamental issues involved in individual choice. Axiomatically, for those who support true freedom of choice, the primary focus is on the individual. Only individuals have rights, and those rights come from our Creator. This is the view enshrined in the founding documents of this nation. All so-called humanistic grounding for rights ultimately unravels due to internal logical contradictions, and then politically unravels, as societies that attempt a secular-based rights scheme degenerate into group-rights warfare. We are headed precisely in that depressing direction today—many would claim that we have already arrived—where only criminals seem to enjoy individual rights against state action. Hyperbole, you say? Let me list some rights—and therefore individual choices—that Americans have foregone: international travel without state harassment; contracts without state mandates; acquisition and disposal of property, domestically and internationally, without state mandates; choosing to spend one's income primarily on oneself; choosing a particular risk-cost trade-off in the products that we buy, our lifestyles, and our work places; access to—and the right to ingest—drugs that we think may be beneficial for us; the right to farm a piece of land, grow what we want, and sell it to whom we please at a mutually agreed upon price; the right to improve our property without state harassment and interventions (an act that today can actually result in prison time for the "offender"); the right to pay, or work, for a mutually agreed wage below the government's so-called minimum; the right to not join a union; virtually any claim to privacy not directly related to sexual or criminal activity, with even those exceptions gradually disappearing. I could continue but, instead, I refer you to those who have already completed more comprehensive examinations, such as James Bovard in his recent book, *Lost Rights.*

The simple, clear, and obvious point is that since the founding of this nation, Americans have ceded a great variety and number of free choice opportunities to the state. In fact, we have ceded so many—and are now so regulated—that we rival, in Nisbet's apt description, inhabitants of medieval society who were "so accustomed to the multitudinous ordinances of the church governing their lives that they didn't even see them." Aren't we more enlightened than those peasants? Nisbet goes on to write that "this is far more true today of modern, democratic man." Today, I accuse Nisbet of understatement!

Opposing the individualistic claim that people are an end in themselves, that they own their own bodies, and that they have the natural right to freedom of action to further their pursuit of happiness is the collectivist vision that argues, essentially, the exact opposite. People, in the collectivist view, are a natural resource that belongs to the state. This is, perhaps, a stark way of asserting their position, but what other conclusion can one draw when confronted with our current legislated policies? Hardly an hour goes by that is not filled with some interest group, academic, or politician arguing that yet another aspect of our freedom be sacrificed to the "public interest," or the "common good," or "to protect our children's future," or the other "usual suspect" gods that collectivists worship. That "great sucking sound," contrary to Ross Perot's claim, is not American jobs leaving for warmer climes. It is the sound of the American freedom to choose being vacuumed away by government.

Typically, these incursions on our freedom of action are argued under the doctrine that economists call cost socialization. Once an undertaking has been collectivized—health care, for example—then any action you may take that might affect another's tax liability becomes justification for the government to curb your choices. I am sure most of you have read a letter to the editor or heard someone make a claim similar to this: "Freedom to not wear a helmet? And who pays for the result? We all do. There is no freedom to do what financially affects other people." At first, this seems a fairly compelling argument. After all, not wearing a helmet is stupid behavior, isn't it? And who opposes outlawing stupid behavior? Especially behavior that may create monetary liabilities for "all of us." It seems a small sacrifice for the nonhelmet wearing public to dispense with their "claimed" freedom to choose in favor of the overwhelming "public good," i.e., protecting lives (whether they want to be protected or not) and "controlling health care costs." But I argue that is the single most pernicious smokescreen yet invented to end your freedom to choose. Taken to its logical conclusion—and many are perfectly willing to go there—it would effectively end both the principle and the practice of individual freedom for there is virtually no action that does not, actually or potentially, affect the position of "the public."

We know, for example, that sexual contact may result in the transmittal of certain diseases. Shouldn't we, therefore, ban all sexual contact that does not follow exacting government-mandated safety standards? After all, such free decisions affect the health care costs of everyone. But, you might say, we can't know that any particular sexual encounter is going to result in a disease being transmitted. It may not, that is true. But we also can't know that any particular motorcycle trip might result in a head injury. It is a statistical tendency—nothing more. And we have statistical tendencies galore for sexual contacts. Same principle. Same standard of evidence. Why not the same policy?

Why do states require driving tests? Because incompetent drivers may impose costs on all of us. (I will set aside the question of whether these state programs actually increase driver competence and will assume, for the sake of argument, that they do.) But is it not true that incompetent parents create situations far more dangerous and costly for us than incompetent drivers? But, you might say, we can't know whether the offspring of incompetent parents are going to be gang members or the next Beethoven, whether they will be a financial burden or turn into brilliant, independent entrepreneurs. But so what? We can't know that a person who has not taken a state driver's test will drive for fifty years without incident—or won't. But statistically . . . well, same principle, same evidence. Many Americans believe that one ought not have children until first satisfying the state as to their competence. And they are perfectly correct, given their socialization of costs argument. But that is an argument that, most of the time, should be categorically rejected. Otherwise, for example, American firms could argue that when consumers shift from American to foreign-made products, our unemployment and welfare costs rise. Should people be allowed to throw their fellow Americans out of work, reduce the equity values of pension funds, create additional welfare support costs? For that matter, why should Texans be allowed to make choices that negatively affect people in Michigan? Or people in Dallas make choices that negatively affect people in Houston? The potential is infinite and dangerous. Not one Framer of our Constitution would believe his eyes were he to see what has already been done in the name of that document—and with the acquiescent support of the majority of America's politically appointed federal judges.

We came within a hair of enacting a form of national health insurance four years ago. The fact is, however, that we have been doing precisely that—piecemeal—for years. But not because the state crammed it down our throats. It happened because Americans no longer believe that in return for individual freedom, people are responsible for the consequences of their choices. If, when you have the freedom to spend your income as you wish, you fail to provide for your health care, under what logically conceivable formulation am I responsible for you when you get sick? People seem to want to believe that "government money" is somehow free. They actually want to be relieved of choice, preferring that the taxpayers clean up the mess. It will not do to argue that such people do not exist and so do not vote in great numbers. What other reason is there to explain the current makeup of Congress except to argue that Americans are, quite simply, morons who cannot differentiate between candidates and therefore get policies they don't really want. I reject that view in favor of the more obvious proposition that, as H. L. Mencken put it, "democracy is the theory that says the common people get to vote for policies and then deserve to get them good and hard."

In my earlier, and pure libertarian, days I used to be skeptical of the argument that freedom requires responsibility and that, if responsibility ceased to be a practiced value, freedom would vanish. Today, I see the great wisdom of this view. Freedom of choice requires a sense of responsibility both to ourselves and to the people with whom we inhabit our cities, states, and nation. (I leave out the rest of the world because I never have cared much for "helping" or "policing" other nations. Such policies merely bring about the growth of the domestic state, along with its control over our lives, as it attempts to control the choices of people in other nations too.) Not buying insurance is an example of freedom without responsibility. Rather than nationalize the entire health care system, why don't we simply require people to have medical insurance, either through their employers (an effect of previous government interventions that time does not permit me to explore) or through their own devices? We could do the same thing with old-age pensions, letting people out of the mandated Social Security system as long as they have "proof of pension." States require people to have automobile insurance when they drive, but states do not provide it nor specify which insurance company.

Why not do the same for health insurance? I suspect that the reason is that so many Americans have accepted the argument that health care is a right—by birth, I assume?—and that they ought not have to pay for it. But they *will* pay for it, of course, and they will pay more and receive worse care if the system is collectivized. (Perhaps it is no longer just people like those in the former Soviet Union who need to be trained in the art of how to make

individual choices? Like staining glass, individual choice, with responsibility, appears to be well on the way to becoming a lost art.)
Nothing that is produced is a right, since someone must be forced
to provide it, and so, for them, the "right" vanishes. Yet such a
preposterous view of rights is gaining ground daily with the electorate as politicians promise more and more free goodies in exchange for votes. As the Framers realized, this has always been the
deadly worm in the apple of democracy.

Before agreeing to restrict our natural freedom to pursue happiness, we ought to ask those who support the collectivist model
the following questions:

*1. Why do you believe that some people know what is better for other people
than those people themselves?*

This looks like an easy one, doesn't it? Anyone who goes to a
doctor reveals that he believes the doctor probably knows what is
better for him than he does himself, right? But begin by asking
yourself a more fundamental question: Why are there doctors in
the first place? Or electricians? Or even economists? Is it not clear
that people, choosing freely over time, have themselves created,
supported, and therefore sustained these professions? Why? Were
we forced by the state? No. We did it, and continue to do it, out of
self-interest. Hence, we rationally understand that no one knows
everything and that each of us, from time to time, requires advice.
Further, just because I consult a podiatrist because my foot hurts
does not logically imply (and, if one researches malpractice cases,
does not empirically imply) that the doctor knows what is best for
me. Experts do exist and they are valuable. Do they therefore
know what is good for other people generally? *Absolutely not.* Since
humans are fallible, it would be best to confine the adverse consequences of a mistake to the person who made it. Having people in
power make choices for everyone leads to collective disasters.
There is, of course, a related difficulty here. What is going to be
your "stopping rule?" That is: if you know better than I, does that
not imply that someone else knows better than you? And so on? Is
an absolute dictatorship of the most knowledgeable not your obvious logical destination?

2. Assuming that you have demonstrated the possibility of finding the sort of people described in the preceding question, why should those people be allowed to make collective choices?

Assume, for the sake of argument, that you have found a person who not only claims to know what is better for me than I do, but who actually does (in theory). Your job is just beginning because now you have to construct a political theory that demonstrates why this person ought to make my decisions. No political theorist has ever made it past the first question, let alone this one. But let's move on.

3. Assuming, once again for the sake of argument, that someone formulates acceptable answers to Questions 1 and 2, what mechanism guarantees that the person who "knows best" will wind up in power?

Ever since Plato's *Republic,* there has been no shortage of attempts to demonstrate, theoretically, how utopias might come to exist. Yet empirically, the record is devastating to the hopes of those who believe in collective mechanisms. Although one can set up a totalitarian state, no one has ever claimed that such states give power to those who know what is best—unless one wishes to argue that killing tens of millions of people was good for them, and that these policies set a good precedent for future decision making! This last hurdle is why so many collectivist utopians have written so much about how a human's nature—once their pet system exists—will "fundamentally change." This is a backhanded compliment to capitalism as it suggests that capitalism is based, at least currently, on human nature. It also demonstrates the lengths to which one has to go in order to deal with the problems raised by the above questions. Of course, if people are going to be other than we have always known them to be, then any claimed system is theoretically workable since these human nature changes can always exist in some author's "theoretically possible" future.

Over the many years that I have been offering this three-question, extra-credit research project to my students who claim to prefer collective choice to individual choice, I have never awarded one extra-credit point. The simple reason is that not one student ever finished the project with answers that appeared remotely reasonable—to the student! The more one thinks about this issue, the more pro-individualist one typically becomes. It is just that most of us do not think about it enough, and students typically are never encouraged to question the collectivist biases in their textbooks, or the stale and musty myths and concomitant sloppy logic that permeate the minds of their teachers.

In the same vein, politics does not challenge us to think so much as it tempts us to abandon rational thought altogether in deference to intentions, compassion, and feeling good about ourselves. This tendency has been analyzed brilliantly by Thomas Sowell in his 1995 book, *The Vision of the Anointed.* Politically, it appears that one is judged more often by one's intentions than by the results of one's policies. Much too often, it seems, reason is trumped by emotion. Our pop public educational philosophy slowly is transforming our political reality as the graduates of its emotion-driven educational philosophy age and start voting—and this is destroying us. One day—*and one vote*—at a time.

Is there any role, then, for collective decisionmaking? Am I suggesting by my title that I endorse anarchy? No. I believe in a public sector that sets reasonable and necessary rules of procedure, and arrests and punishes those who violate those rules. I believe in a public sector that defends the nation. By that, I do not mean a defense establishment that undertakes one extra-domestic military adventure after another, all in the name of defending America. If Congress is unwilling to declare war, in my view we ought not to be militarily involved. That was fairly obvious to the Framers, and was the majority opinion in the nation for some time. Today, I guess it places me in the "extreme" camp with the old, dead (small "r") republican stalwarts like Garet Garrett. So be it. In my minority view, there is even a role for national and state governments in environmental control. I do not agree with the libertarian "solutions" to some pollution problems thus far advanced, even in theory. This is a classic public goods problem, and it deserves the most serious and careful regulation. Of course, the chance of getting that in today's political climate is less than the chance of winning the lottery.

Nonetheless, in theory, there is a role here for useful collective action. I would guess that my version of the federal government might cost about $300 billion a year—about 4 percent of current GNP. This could easily be funded with a combination of court-use fees and a small national sales tax. For that reason, I favor immediate repeal of the Sixteenth Amendment and the addition of *an income tax ban* to the Constitution. I know that even this won't make pure libertarians happy, but a reduction from current spending—about 28 percent of GNP with all the attendant tax distortions and, of course, the beloved IRS—to that small amount, with the abolition of income tax, is more political progress than I will ever see in my lifetime. But life goes on and the future *must* be changed if we are to survive as an economically great nation.

Collective choices must be made at all levels of life. Randian individualists, subject to no one's will but their own, are—and happily so—pure fantasy, although there is, of course, the state of Montana! The difference between private collective choices and government collective choices is that the former are usually exercised within a framework where competitive options exist. If I do not like the outcomes of the collective choices my fellow condominium owners make through our owners' association, I can move. If I don't care for the rules of my bridge club, I can join another or form one of my own. If I don't like the regulations of the Food and Drug Administration, what exactly can I do? The fact is my power to change FDA policy is minuscule. I do have the right to vote. But even the least cynical observer will have to admit that a close examination of government policy in this century suggests that, once enacted, change is virtually impossible. If voting means simply the ability to change politicians and not policy, then voting is worthless.

Of course, if one is blessed with patience—the sort of patience that allows you to enjoy watching stalagmites form—then one might change policy by helping elect presidents who select judges who then ignore existing precedents, and so on. But, of course, I jest.

The above considerations suggest that what we ought to do is widen the scope for individual and private collective choice, as opposed to government-mandated collective choice. This will work, as I have argued above, only insofar as we do not continue to become, again in Nisbet's accurate formulation, a nation of "loose individuals"—obsessed with our right to do whatever we please regardless of the consequences for others, engrossed only in the latest fads, as institutions that are worth saving (such as our colleges and universities) continue to collapse around us.

Individual choice is the foundation of any free society. It is impossible to overestimate its significance and, for that reason, it is easy to see why it is under assault from every public or private organization that wants to transform this nation into a collective entity along the lines of the European socialist welfare states—or worse. Lysander Spooner's observation that "vices are not crimes" seems to fall on an ever-larger number of deaf ears in this country. Some group—and not always the government, but usually committed to the "government as an instrument of salvation" viewpoint—wants to deny you choice in virtually every area of your life. And, of course, all this is being advocated and legislatively enacted "for your own good."

Individuals cannot be trusted, but collective interest groups can choose rationally. How allegedly irrational individuals become rational when they join together is an assumption seldom investigated. Yet *you* should investigate it within the context of the three questions I put forward earlier. It will be difficult, however, since anti-choice interest groups and their government allies have an effective weapon with which to deal with dissent: They brand all such resistance to their pet policy proposals as the pleadings of "special interests." This gives the media the option to pick and choose which groups are to be denigrated—and hence dismissed— by the use of this loaded terminology. The NRA? Definitely a special interest. The Christian Coalition? Definitely. Public Citizen? No, that is a "public interest" organization.

Having labeled their pets as working for the "public good," and their political enemies as being merely "special interests," the media can then simply ignore public pronouncements of the latter while trumpeting the press releases of the former. No matter how silly and inaccurate the so-called "studies" that such groups release are—for example, the Natural Resources Defense Council's Alar scare, or the silliness over Olestra and burning churches—the next time approved groups sound off, one can expect the media to roll over and jump through the usual hoops. They did so again last May when the NRDC released its latest air pollution "study." The irresponsible manner in which the media cover these stories is one of the great intellectual scandals of our age, and contributes as much as anything to the reduced faith in individual choice. The fact is that all such collectives are special interest groups, regardless of their claims, and all should be treated equally. Further, their so-called studies ought to be subjected to careful scrutiny and scientific peer review in reputable journals before their contentions are even reported.

Virtually every practice is under attack by America's anti-individual choice puritans and Thought Police. Your choice to drive a car, wear leather or fur, eat certain foods, drink alcohol, smoke tobacco, choose your employees or friends, choose your drug or medical care options, wear perfumes and colognes, have a pet. . . . When the state attempts to forbid behavior that is widely practiced and popular, it creates laws that inspire contempt, are routinely disobeyed, and corrupt its police and courts.

The costs of these follies are well-documented. The rise of organized crime during the 1920s while the Volstead Act was enforced coincided with a period of increasing alcohol consumption by the young. The horribly expensive, corrupting, and, thus far, futile War on Drugs, has brought staggering costs in prisons, extra bureaucracy, police corruption, sacrificed liberty, ridicule for the Rule of Law, and gross violations of private property rights. (Prisons are full of people jailed for "possession," while the wealthy—famous actors or athletes—are never incarcerated. And public officials routinely use, or have used, the same drugs themselves.)

There is no shortage of examples of what special interest-group lobbies create once their cherished prohibitions are enacted into law. The mystery is: Why do so many believe that—next time—the results will be different? When people don't agree with laws, even when they are intellectually defensible, it is useless to waste time and money on prosecutions. That is why Jack Kervorkian is not in prison and is unlikely to ever be. It is a simple lesson, but one that seems to require periodic relearning. Unfortunately, the ones who learn, typically, are not the fervid fanatics who wish to criminalize virtually all of human choice and, therefore, human existence. It is the rest of us who pay the price for their follies while they are lauded by the media, worshipped by members in their own narrow special interest milieu, and usually wind up having freeways or government buildings named after them, and sycophantic television or Hollywood movies made about their lives—lives spent meddling in other peoples' business.

The rebirth of liberty in this nation must be led by a rebirth in the freedom of individuals to choose. To suggest that freedom has been expanded by our increasingly regulated environment proscribing certain individual choices is as intellectually dishonest, and as factually incorrect, as any political argument ever advanced. It is arguable that, as a move is made from anarchy to limited government, overall freedom may well be enhanced.

However, my contention is that government regulations reach a potential, or theoretic, "freedom maximization point" rather quickly before diminishing returns set in. If this vision (that increasing the number of regulations increases human freedom) is accepted, as were the myriad regulations of the medieval church, it will become so interwoven into our lives that we will believe it to be true—then we can bid farewell to what remains of the American experiment with political freedom and individual choice.

May that day never arrive. Instead, let us proclaim, with both logic and history on our side: "Laissez-faire. Let individuals choose."

Works Cited

Bovard, James. 1994. *Lost Rights.* (New York: St. Martin's Press).

Nisbet, Robert. 1988. *The Present Age: Progress and Anarchy in Modern America.* (New York: Harper and Row).

Sacks, David O., and Peter Thiel. 1995. *The Diversity Myth: "Multiculturalism" and the Politics of Intolerance at Stanford.* (Oakland, CA: Independent Institute).

Sowell, Thomas. 1995. *The Vision of the Anointed.* (New York: Basic Books).

Disclaimer: The views expressed in this essay are solely those of the author and do not necessarily reflect those of either the Federal Reserve Bank of Dallas or the Federal Reserve System.

The Constitution and Commerce: The Case for Self-Government

There are laws of physics, laws of health, economic laws, laws of chemistry, and laws of God. Societal mores can govern. In business one soon learns that the customer often rules. "Government is everywhere," and we should be grateful that in the end God governs in the affairs of men.

Noting that most government is not what we call civil government, the question is, then, in relations between man and man, who or what should govern?

I suggest that the morally highest form of human government is self-government: the individual's free-will obedience to divine law. A near second is the government of the family, for it is there that individual self-government is best taught, learned, and nurtured.

Civil government is the crudest, or lowest, form of government—speaking in the moral sense now—because civil government has as its primary tools force and compulsion. Civil government is necessary, but it should always be the last resort. The greater the self-discipline of a people, the less external civil government is necessary.

James Madison noted in *The Federalist* that the writers of the Constitution chose "to rest all our political experiments on the capacity of mankind for self-government." Such men as John Adams and George Washington were even more specific, arguing that a free society depended on citizens who were religious and God-fearing. The Founders generally shared the notion that there was a higher law above all the acts of political councils to which nations must someday give account; when any people put their own will above that of the revelations of God, bondage and suffering would be the end result. Therefore, only the God-fearing would be self-governing.

The Founders did not trust human nature. With a few notable exceptions, they shared a passionate distrust for the democracy of the French Revolution, which was an expression of the unbridled will of the people and which sought to institute an all-powerful secular state that could "perfect" its subjects. The Christian concept of man embraced by American colonial leaders was that man was fallen, very capable of evil, and his only salvation was to "get religion" and be changed by the power of the redemption of Jesus Christ.[1] Those noble men, whom constitutional convention delegate William Pierce called "the wisest Council in all the World,"[2] understood the capacity of man to do good—and the propensity of man to do evil. Citizens in political office were not to be trusted any more than citizens out of office, as that trust pertains to the exercise of power over another. Therefore, the Constitution was crafted to check the weaknesses of man's nature, to let the best in man shine forth and the worse be restrained. Thus, the Founders had greater trust in individual freedom than in centralized government. This system of checks and balances that they devised is perhaps the Constitution's most magnificent yet unappreciated feature.

Madison wrote in a later number of *The Federalist* [Nr. 51]:

Ambition must be made to counteract ambition. . . . It may be a reflection on human nature, that such devices should be necessary to control the abuses of government. But what is government itself, but the greatest of all reflections on human nature? If men were angels, no government would be necessary. [No civil government, that is.] If angels were to govern men, neither external nor internal controls of government would be necessary. In framing a government which is to be administered by men over men, the great difficulty lies in this: you must first enable the government to control the governed; and in the next place oblige it to control itself.

One man by himself is limited in the harm he can do, but given political power, that same man can destroy entire nations.

Powers Given to Congress

Article I, Section 1 of the Constitution reads:

> *All legislative Powers herein granted shall be vested in a Congress of the United States, which shall consist of a Senate and House of Representatives.*

That simple statement means that only Congress is endowed with the power to make law—not the courts and certainly not the executive branch. Section 8 of Article I contains the key elements which give the government the power over our lives and commercial endeavors. It begins:

> *The Congress shall have Power to lay and collect taxes, duties, imposts and excises.*

Money being the fuel of government, it should come as no surprise that a government charter would first list the power to exact funds from the citizenry. The Founders had learned from the Articles of Confederation that the absence of an enforceable taxing structure makes a national government a farce. So, like it or not, government must tax us, and it is the job of Congress to decide what and how much to tax.

The next phrases refer to the purpose of taxation, essentially limiting taxing powers and requiring the uniform application of taxes across the nation. Needed funds not raised by taxes may be borrowed, but the Framers never intended that the national government force anyone to become a lender. Indeed, the power to make "bills of credit"—paper money—a legal tender was struck from a draft of the Constitution at the Constitutional Convention, and that power was neither enumerated nor implied. Unfortunately, this understanding was lost during the Civil War.

The very next grant listed was "to regulate commerce among the several states," which we will return to later. The balance of Section 8 empowered Congress to make provisions for establishing an environment in which the people could prosper. Congress then established a language of commerce: rules pertaining to bankruptcies, the establishment of a monetary system, and standards of weights and measures. Imagine how difficult it would be if everyone defined a pound or an inch or a dollar differently.

The Constitution permits the construction of post offices and roads for conveying the post. This was not an exclusive grant of power, but in the late 1800s with the help of the courts, Congress usurped that power and forbade competition. Only recently, through the advances of transportation and communication technologies, has this monopoly been cracked. E-mail, the fax machine, and overnight express mail have reopened the free market for first-class mail. Postal authorities have yet to figure out how to get the cat back in the bag, but they are trying.

Next is the protection of intellectual property with the power to grant patents and copyrights. Where would the software and music industries be without the help of copyrights?

Section 8 also provides for the establishment of a court system to enforce contracts and punish crime. Congress was granted the power to protect trade from pirates on land or sea and also given war-making powers.

For the most part, our national government has restrained its use of these powers, especially when compared with other nations. An exception, however, is the money system. Our current monetary system is a house of cards precisely because we have abandoned the Constitution in this area.

The Commerce Clause

Now we will return to the commerce clause, the single most troubling source of governmental abuse. This short statement was inserted immediately following the power to borrow money. Here Congress was given power

> to regulate commerce with foreign nations, and among the several states and with the Indian tribes.

We will examine this clause in relation only to commerce "among the several states," which has been the justification for labor laws, the minimum wage, the Occupational Safety and Health Administration, the Environmental Protection Agency, the Food and Drug Administration, health care regulations, truth-in-packaging, and so forth. It is in this arena that over the past sixty years the powers of government have grown beyond imagination—and become exceedingly noxious. It is the excuse for intrusion into our businesses, backyards, and homes. Though welfare/transfer payments have become the biggest expense of government, it is the contorted application of the commerce clause that has given license to the federal government to become dictatorial in style, and arbitrary and capricious in policy.

Let's look at the origins of the commerce clause and the reasons for vesting these and related powers in a central government.

Remember that the thirteen original states had been independent and somewhat competitive colonies. They felt little allegiance to each other until abuses from the British Crown caused them to unite to defend themselves. Commerce tended to be between England and the colonies more than among the colonies themselves. England had the manufacturers and the colonies had the raw materials. As the colonies grew in population, indigenous manufacturing increased. Compared to the population of England, the colonists were rich: They could own their own homes, work their own fields, and build their own ships.

Eighteenth-century England, you will recall, was still operating under a mercantilist system where certain powerful business interests, often owned by members of the nobility, monopolized commerce. Privileges in the form of exclusive licenses were granted by the Crown to the chosen few in exchange for taxes. It is easier to collect taxes from one monopoly than from hundreds of small businesses. The common man was a tenant because most land was owned by the Crown or other nobility.

Americans were more free than their overseas relatives because they were physically distant. Forced to take care of themselves, they became fiercely independent.

As Parliament and the Crown sought to exercise the same kind of control over the colonies that was the norm in Britain, the colonists resisted. It was an assault on the freedom they had come to enjoy.

During the War for Independence, the colonies united to fight a war—not to create an enduring nation. So naturally, in our first constitution, the Articles of Confederation, the national government was nothing but a loose confederation born of necessity. When the war was over, the general attitude was one of gratitude,

"But now let's get back to work." The framework of state government already existed, but the concept of a national government was not really welcomed nor trusted. After all, hadn't they just fought a war against a strong central government? Therefore, the states became provincial and rivalries and jealousies abounded.

The great legal scholar Joseph Story—a contemporary of the signers, the first dean of the Harvard Law School, and a member of the Supreme Court—wrote his first definitive commentary on the Constitution in 1833.[3] It is a classic, and perhaps the best source we have for determining the intended interpretation and application of the Constitution. Justice Story wrote:

> It is hardly possible to exaggerate the oppressed and degraded state of domestic commerce, manufactures, and agriculture at the time of the adoption of the Constitution. Our ships were almost driven from the ocean; our work-shops were nearly deserted; our mechanics were in a starving condition; and our agriculture was sunk to the lowest ebb. These were the natural results of the inability of the General Government to regulate commerce, so as to prevent the injurious monopolies and exclusions of foreign nations, and the conflicting and often ruinous regulations of the different states.[4]

The only way to unite the states for their mutual benefit was to reduce the barriers for commercial and social intercourse among the people of the states. Free and vigorous commerce among the people was also necessary to strengthen and sustain their independence. It was in this spirit that the writers of the Constitution determined to vest in a national government an exclusive power over commerce between the states. Thus so many of the powers granted to Congress by the Constitution were to promote a vigorous and free economy.

What does it mean to regulate commerce? Here I refer to Noah Webster's original 1828 dictionary,[5] which represents the language used in the constitutional period. (In fact, many words were defined by referencing scripture or the Constitution as illustrations of proper usage.)

"To regulate," according to Webster, meant to "adjust by rule, method or established mode . . . to put in good order . . . to subject to rules or restrictions." "Commerce" was defined as the trafficking of goods, buying, selling, and transporting of goods, persons or messages. Commerce was not to be confused with manufacturing nor agriculture.

Manufacturing is done in a specific locale while commerce connotes movement, which may be across state borders. The constitutional language in this clause restricts itself to the regulation of commerce crossing state borders and does not address manufacturing. But today we confuse the words and assume that commerce also includes the concept of manufacturing. Joseph Story insisted upon the distinction in his *Commentaries.*

> Are not commerce and manufactures as distinct, as commerce and agriculture? If they are, how can a power to regulate one arise from a power to regulate the other? . . . If this were admitted, the enumeration of the powers of Congress would be wholly unnecessary and nugatory. Agriculture, colonies, capital, machinery, the wages of labour, the profits of stock, the rents of land . . . would all be within the scope of the power; for all of them bear an intimate relation to commerce. . . . The power to regulate manufactures is no more confided to Congress, than the power to interfere with the systems of education, the poor laws, or the road laws of the states. It is notorious, that, in the convention, an attempt was made to introduce into the Constitution a power to encourage manufactures; but it was withheld.[6]

To regulate commerce among the several states, then, means to establish rules and regulations for the orderly trafficking of goods, services, and communications moving across state lines. Sadly, what Justice Story rejected is now the common interpretation of the courts. Congress does now exercise power over wages, over agriculture, over education.

Limited Government vs. Government Without Limits

How did we take this path from limited government to government without limits?

Usurpation of power by government is often accomplished under the guise of necessity. And what greater necessity is there than survival? For example, wartime measures justified the issuing of paper money as legal tender, justified wage and price controls, and justified federal intrusion into education.

Another growth area in federal commerce regulations came with ambitious western expansion and the granting of special monopolistic privileges to railroads. With those favors granted to a select few, commensurate regulation followed as a natural consequence. One abuse of power justified another.

An additional catalyst for government intrusion has come from certain commercial interests seeking to restrain competition or gain personal advantage by lobbying to regulate their industry or receive subsidies. The Food and Drug Administration, for example, is used by large medical concerns to frustrate their competition.

The problem of one expansion of power necessitating another has been a known method of revolution. Karl Marx knew that the socializing of the West would be difficult. He proposed

> . . . in the beginning, this [socializing of the West] cannot be effected except by means of despotic inroads on the rights of property . . . by means of measures, therefore, which appear economically insufficient and untenable, but which in the course of the movement, outstrip themselves, necessitate further inroads upon the old social order and are unavoidable as a means of entirely revolutionizing the mode of production.[9]

In 1913, Congress passed the Federal Reserve Act establishing a national banking system. (Marx had advocated the centralization of credit in the hands of government.) Though clearly unconstitutional, the act was passed the day before Christmas recess when members of Congress were eager to catch the train home. A cushy deal between government and powerful banking interests, it made what we now call the monetizing of debt possible by allowing the conversion of federal debt into circulating Federal Reserve notes with legal tender status. These notes were first backed by a partial reserve of gold, then the conversion price was diluted, and finally the precious metal backing was completely removed.

Also during 1913, the Sixteenth Amendment—the income tax amendment—was approved by the states, giving the national government the power to tax income from whatever source and to whatever degree. With these new powers, Congress now had the fiscal muscle to buy votes, buy property, erect enterprises, do public works. And if taxes were insufficient, through the Federal Reserve System it could force the citizens to lend money to the government. The way was paved for government to compete with private enterprise.

In 1913, the Seventeenth Amendment was adopted as well, which changed the manner of election to the Senate. Originally, senators were elected by state legislatures which protected the interests and prerogatives of the states. This was a vital check on the expansion of federal power. This change to the direct election of senators broke down an important barrier to federal intrusion.

All in all, 1913 was not a good year for the cause of freedom in this country.

Another turning point came during the Franklin Roosevelt era when the scope of government exploded the chains that the Constitution had placed on it. The necessity this time was not war initially, but financial turmoil and the Great Depression. The Depression was due in large measure to the financial excesses made possible by the Federal Reserve System which, when the "Fed" reversed its course, precipitated the market crash and the implosion of the banking system. Unfortunately, the cure was not to revoke old unconstitutional acts but to add even more powers to government. During those years of economic emergency, the federal government dramatically expanded its powers, and the courts eventually gave in. Because Congress cannot pass regulations fast enough, it has mainly delegated this authority to the executive branch. The legislative power constitutionally vested solely in Congress is now assumed primarily by executive boards, commissions, and agencies.

"To regulate commerce among the several states" was never intended to mean to establish and operate businesses such as the Tennessee Valley Authority, the Federal Reserve System, insurance companies, and railroad lines.

There are some proper examples of federal regulation. One is the regulation of the airwaves, radio and TV, cellular and satellite. Without reasonable regulation as to who may use which frequencies, we would have all kinds of chaos and piracy. In this area, too, some regulations have been excessive, but the power to regulate this activity is clearly within the scope of the Constitution. Proper regulation makes commerce over the air much more feasible, just as a rule requiring drivers to use the right-hand side of the road brings order and safety—and actually increases freedom.

Moral Courage

We live in a constitutional republic, a form of government wherein the people exercise sovereignty through their elected representatives according to the rules and limitations written into their political charter. This means that if those we elect go astray, we the people have responsibility to correct them.

Why is it that today we are so good at complaining about government, but actually do so little to change it? Is it ignorance, apathy, impotence, or some other inherent weakness in the population? I would suggest that the core reason for electoral impotence is the absence of moral courage.

Let me quote the venerable Benjamin Franklin on the occasion of the signing of the Constitution in 1787. In endorsing the document, Franklin said:

> . . . I agree to this Constitution with all its faults, if they are such; because I think a general Government necessary for us, and there is no form of Government but what may be a blessing to the people if well administered, and believe farther that this is likely to be well administered for a course of years and can only end in Despotism, as other forms have done before it, when the people shall become so corrupted as to need despotic Government, being incapable of any other.[8]

My conviction is that prosperity results from our being a God-fearing and virtuous people. If our focus were on material prosperity only, to the exclusion of virtue, in time we would have neither. It is the absence of virtue that breeds government expansion because there is no moral courage to resist it.

But not all trends are toward tyranny. While the "feds" are going strong in health care, environmental, labor and workplace law, we have seen encouraging progress away from overbearing regulations in the public utilities, transportation, banking, and communications.

The satellite dish, the Internet, and computers also allow the individual to react faster than government can. It is as if government policymakers are now scurrying behind the crowd shouting, "Wait for me, I'm your regulator!"

Technology has increased freedom and the need for virtue and self-government because technology has increased our capacities to do both good and ill.

Justice Story concluded his *Commentaries* with these thoughts:

> Let the American youth never forget, that they possess a noble inheritance, bought by the toils, and sufferings, and blood of their ancestors; and capable, if wisely improved, and faithfully guarded, of transmitting to their latest posterity all the substantial blessings of life, the peaceful enjoyment of liberty, property, religion, and independence. . . . It may, nevertheless, perish in an hour by the folly, or corruption, or negligence of its only keepers, THE PEOPLE. Republics are created by the virtue, public spirit, and intelligence of the citizens. They fall, when the wise are banished from the public councils, because they dare to be honest, and the profligate are rewarded, because they flatter the people, in order to betray them.[9]

So now we are back to where we began. The highest form of government is self-government—our free-will obedience to divine law. If we are to enjoy freedom for ourselves and our posterity, then we as a nation must turn again to the grantor of all good gifts, put our lives in harmony with His will, and spread His message so others will learn. This effort must begin in the home where truth must be taught and self-government learned.

The Lord in Old Testament times promised his children:

If my people, which are called by my name, shall humble
themselves, and pray, and seek my face, and turn from their
wicked ways; then will I hear from heaven, and will forgive
their sin, and will heal their land. [2 Chronicles 7:14]

If we learn to govern ourselves we too can experience that healing.

Notes

[1]See George Washington's "Farewell Address."
[2]Charles Callan Tansill, Ed., *The Making of the American Republic: The Great
Documents: 1774–1789* (New Rochelle, NY: Arlington House, 1972), 108.
[3]Joseph Story, *Commentaries on the Constitution of the United States*, Vols. I–III
[1833] (New York: Da Capo Press, 1970).
[4]Joseph Story, *A Familiar Exposition of the Constitution of the United States* [1840]
(Lake Bluffs, IL: Regnery Gateway, 1986), 140.
[5]Noah Webster, *An American Dictionary of the English Language* [1828] (Ana-
heim, CA: Foundation for American Christian Education, 1967).
[6]*Commentaries*, Vol. II, 521–22.
[7]*The Communist Manifesto* (Chicago: Henry Regnery, 1954), 54.
[8]From James Madison's notes from the Convention of 1787. See Charles
Callan Tansill, 739.
[9]*Commentaries*, Vol. III, 759–60.

HARRY BROWNE

Too Many Lawyers
or Too Many Laws?

Government doesn't work, as we have all figured out by now. It can't deliver the mail on time, it doesn't educate our children properly, it doesn't keep our cities safe. Yet a gigantic game of "Let's Pretend" goes on. Let's pretend the War on Poverty really does help poor people. Let's pretend the War on Drugs really does something about drugs in America and really does reduce crime.

Government has failed at practically everything that it does, but it is good at one thing. It knows how to break your legs, cripple you, and then hand you a crutch and say, "See, if it weren't for the government you wouldn't be able to walk." It is destroying health care in America through Medicare and Medicaid, and then it says, "See, if it weren't for the government you wouldn't be able to get medical care and you'd probably be dying in the streets." It has created a situation where people everywhere have become dependent upon the government because of the problems that government itself has created.

But it has also perfected the knack of blaming others for the sins of government. Government destroyed the health care system, but who are we mad at? The health insurance companies. In the 1970s we had rampant inflation in America, but who got the blame? Arab oil sheiks and labor unions and "greedy" businessmen. No one blamed the government's loose monetary policy, which had been allowed to eat away at the economy for ten years and which had made inflation inevitable.

Government always finds a scapegoat, somebody to blame. Thus we never have to face the fact that government doesn't work and that what we need to do is reduce government involvement in our lives.

Nowhere can we see this more clearly than with the law today. There is a widespread attitude that the law has been perverted by lawyers. Lawyers take the brunt of all the criticisms, yet the problems with the law have no more to do with lawyers than the health care situation has to do with health insurance companies. *It is a problem of government.* The government has created an environment where the proliferation of lawyers and the aggressiveness of lawyers is the inevitable result.

One consequence of our feelings about law and lawyers is that we have come to believe that we don't have enough government—and that's why we have so much crime in this country today. Conservatives, for instance, say that we need tort reform. What does tort reform mean to them? It means that we need the government to impose laws that say that people can't get more than X number of dollars if they win a lawsuit. Since the government created these lawsuits in the first place, why would we turn to them to solve the problem? And why would we think that adding yet another law to the pile is somehow going to solve it? What we really need, say conservatives, are tougher sentences, more prisons, more police, and mandatory sentences. We need to get tough on criminals, and some even suggest that we need to suspend the bill of rights in some cases in order to put these people behind bars.

How did we get into this position and how might we be able to extricate ourselves? Lawsuits proliferate today because government has created so many laws. Now there's a principle at work here that we may need to consider. Whenever you see a widespread increase in something, you have to ask yourself, "Why is that happening now? It didn't happen before."

For example, people wonder why American companies are moving offshore. Is it because they are greedy and want to increase profits by using low-wage foreign workers? And how can they condone that when American workers are being laid off at an unbelievable rate? Well, companies have always tried to maximize their profits. Companies have always tried to lower their costs in whatever way they could. They are obliged to increase their income in order to increase profits for their shareholders. So why didn't they do this in the 1950s and the 1960s? In the 1950s, they could move

offshore and hire Thai or Indonesian or Korean workers for ten
cents an hour, but companies didn't do it. Why are they doing it
now?

What has happened, obviously, is that we have finally reached
the point where regulations are so oppressive and taxes so high
that American companies have no choice but leave. Low-cost
labor is not the be-all-and-end-all of business. Regulations have
been piled on one by one over the years—the Americans with Disabilities Act, the Civil Rights Act, the Clean Air Act, the Clean Water
Act—every one with a high-sounding purpose, every one to ac-
complish some great social good. Each has added another straw
to the camel's back, and each has increased the opportunity to
sue someone.

The Americans with Disabilities Act, for instance, contains
numerous provisions by which private individuals can sue companies. Every environmental law does the same. Recently, a new set
of regulations was proposed in which companies must submit their
plans to change production methods to the Environmental Protection Agency to make sure that the new method will not, in some
way, lead to pollution. This means that a company like Intel—the
world's largest manufacturer of semiconductor chips, which changes its production practices once or twice a week—will have to submit those plans to the EPA, let the EPA sit on them for sixty days,
then have a public hearing, let the public comment for about sixty days, and then finally, maybe, receive approval. (Of course, by
this time the competition will have moved well ahead.) However,
even if the EPA approves the plan, any private organization or
individual can sue if it believes that Intel is polluting with its new
production process.

Now what this leads to, basically, is a fund-raising scheme for
private organizations. You simply go to a company like Intel and
say you are going to sue because you think its production processes pollute. The result is that Intel has to settle out of court; it simply cannot let production be delayed any longer. Lawyers are at
work here, of course, but the lawyers are not the problem: The
problem is the law that created an opportunity to blackmail.

Texaco recently settled a proposed suit claiming racial discrimination. By the time all the facts had come out, it was obvious
that there had been no racial discrimination. But because the

planned lawsuit would have tied up Texaco in the courts for years, the company simply settled—for $175 million.

We can say that lawyers are preying on us, but are they preying on us any more than college students who accept Pell Grants and student loans from the government? Are they preying on us any more than farmers who accept farm subsidies? Or Archer Daniels Midland who accepts an ethanol subsidy? Or anybody else who takes money from the government or takes advantage of a special privilege? The point is that the laws have created the problems. If we reduce the number of laws, if we eliminate this tangle of regulations, then we will no longer have a litigious society.

The same is true of crime. I grew up in a suburb of Los Angeles. On Friday nights when I was ten or so, I used to walk to the movie theater a mile away, see a movie, and walk home at ten o'clock at night. I had no fear whatsoever of muggers, there were no drug dealers on the street, there were no addicts, there were no homeless people, there were no gangs fighting over monopoly territories.

Crime has reached such a scale that people who believe in the Bill of Rights—people who believe, in theory, in liberty and freedom and individual rights— are willing to sacrifice those things if that is what is necessary to do something about crime. But, again, what has caused this change? Have people suddenly become more evil? Has morality dwindled? I don't think so. People can live under the worst conditions and it won't change their morality. But something has changed and, again, we have to look to the government.

Forty or fifty years ago, police forces, courts, and governments weren't so concerned about victimless crimes—a "crime" for which there is no victim making a complaint. It might involve prostitution, drugs, gambling, or anything that is technically illegal, but where no other human being or property is being trespassed against. Now somebody may report such a crime to the police, but that person is not a victim: He is an informer.

Years ago we had laws against prostitution, drugs, and gambling, but they were enforced mainly in the breech. Drug laws, in particular, were not enforced strongly at all. The first drug law in this country, the Harrison Act, was enacted in 1914. Before 1914, a ten-year-old child could walk into a drugstore and buy heroin right off the shelf, without a prescription, with a note from parents. (It was sold packaged as a pain reliever and a sedative, just as aspirin is today.) And yet despite this unrestricted availability of heroin, there was no drug problem in America. The laws were not enforced and there were no drug problems. But along about 1960, the federal government declared war on drugs, and then we had a drug problem. Once the war on drugs started, they became a criminal enterprise—with black markets.

We are experiencing the second bout of prohibition in America. The first bout occurred during the 1920s when alcohol was illegal and we had gangs fighting over monopoly territories, killings on the street, drive-by shootings—all the things we take for granted today. When prohibition was repealed in 1933, the crime rate in America peaked (after rising for fifteen years) and it fell steadily every year for thirty years—until the war on drugs started.

Now, here again, we have a situation that the government has created—a gigantic criminal drug enterprise where people now have an incentive to hook children on drugs, where people have an incentive to push drugs in your face, hoping you will become a $100-a-day customer for the rest of your short life.

So, what solutions are we offered? Some think we ought to execute all drug dealers. Others say we need to get rid of the exclusionary laws that taint evidence that has been "illegally" obtained and thus can't be used in court. Others think we need mandatory sentences. Others think we need to build more prisons. What is wrong with these suggestions? They all call for more government, which obviously isn't the answer.

Today we have a situation in which murderers, muggers, child molesters, and rapists get out of prison on early release (or they never go in the first place) because there isn't enough room. Why? Because there are marijuana smokers—people who have never committed a violent act against anyone—sitting in those prisons.

I am not saying that all those in prison today are nonviolent. But the point is that 100,000 people convicted of child molestation have received early release from prison because of prison overcrowding. At the same time, more than 100,000 people are sitting in prison today who have never committed a crime of violence, who have never stolen property. Their only crimes are crimes against the state.

We don't need mandatory minimum sentences. We don't need more prisons. We need to focus the law once more on the protection of property and the protection of individuals. Frederic Bastiat, a nineteenth-century French parlimentarian, defined two kinds of laws. If a law is designed to protect life and property, it is a good law in his view. If the law is designed to either take from one and give to another, or to simply enforce one person's will upon another (which is what victimless crime laws do), then it is a bad law.

And what happens when you create bad laws? The law becomes perverted. Resources that should be spent to protect us and our property are being devoted to stamping out vice. And respect for the law itself becomes so diminished that eventually laws have no meaning anymore. The law is no longer the impartial guardian of our liberty, life, and property; now it has become simply an instrument by which one person forces his will upon another. This is why we have a $1.6 trillion government and a $5 trillion debt. That is why the courts are clogged with frivolous lawsuits. That is why we have lawsuits that make people instant millionaires just because they didn't follow the directions on the can or they tried to do something foolish with a ladder.

We have reached the point today where people despair that this insanity will ever end. I don't share their despair. Did you know that polls indicate that 75 percent of the American people think that government is too big? That 62 percent think that it poses an immediate danger to the future of America? That in 1994 when Gallup classified people according to their answers (not by self-labels), they found that 30 percent were conservatives (who wanted more government control over society, but less over the economy), 16 percent were liberals (who wanted more government control over the economy, but less over society), and 20 percent were populists (people who wanted more government control of the economy and of society). Interestingly, 22 percent were libertarians, those who wanted less government control in both our social and economic lives.

What has been missing has been a political channel through which people could funnel their anti-government sentiment. The

Republican Party once seemed to be the proper repository, but it has provided absolutely nothing since winning Congress, just as it provided nothing when it had the presidency. Unfortunately, the Libertarian Party is hardly known to most Americans who feel this great sense of despair. In my view, it will remain that way until there is a political force large enough to be encouraging, to make people feel they can make a difference. Now you may think that means reforming the Republican Party or the Democratic Party. I feel that the best hope is the Libertarian Party because it is growing rapidly and it is focused on the one task of increasing liberty and personal responsibility.

An anti-government movement is building and we have to encourage it. If we do, I believe we can restore the ideas that made America unique—limited government with an impartial law. That was—and remains—the American ideal.

STEPHEN MOORE

Our Unconstitutional Congress

In 1800, when the nation's capital was moved from Philadelphia to Washington, D.C., all of the paperwork and records of the United States government were packed into twelve boxes and then transported the one hundred and fifty miles to Washington in a horse and buggy. That was truly an era of lean and efficient government.

In the early years of the Republic, government bore no resemblance to the colossal empire it has evolved into today. In 1800, the federal government employed three thousand people and had a budget of less than $1 million ($100 million in today's dollars). That's a far cry from today's federal budget of $1.6 trillion and total government workforce of eighteen million.

Since its frugal beginnings, the U.S. federal government has come to subsidize everything from Belgian endive research to maple syrup production to the advertising of commercial brand names in Europe and Japan. In a recent moment of high drama before the Supreme Court, during oral arguments involving the application of the interstate commerce clause of the Constitution, a bewildered Justice Antonin Scalia pressed the solicitor general to name a single activity or program that our modern-day Congress might undertake that would fall outside the bounds of the Constitution. The stunned Clinton appointee could not think of one.

A version of this presentation originally appeared in the Spring 1995 issue of *Policy Review.* Special thanks go to Roger Pilon, director of constitutional studies at the Cato Institute, for his contributions.

During the debate in Congress over the controversial 1994 Crime Bill, not a single Republican or Democrat challenged the $10 billion in social spending on the grounds that it was meant to pay for programs that were not the proper responsibility of the federal government. No one asked, for example, where is the authority under the Constitution for Congress to spend money on midnight basketball, modern dance classes, self-esteem training, and the construction of swimming pools? Certainly, there was plenty of concern about "wasteful spending," but none about unconstitutional spending.

Most federal spending today falls in this latter category because it lies outside Congress's spending powers under the Constitution and it represents a radical departure from the past. For the first one hundred years of our nation's history, proponents of limited government in Congress and the White House routinely argued—with great success—a philosophical and legal case against the creation and expansion of federal social welfare programs.

A Rulebook for Government

The U.S. Constitution is fundamentally a rulebook for government. Its guiding principle is the idea that the state is a source of corruptive power and ultimate tyranny. Washington's responsibilities were confined to a few enumerated powers, involving mainly national security and public safety. In the realm of domestic affairs, the Founders sought to guarantee that federal interference in the daily lives of citizens would be strictly limited. They also wanted to make sure that the minimal government role in the domestic economy would be financed and delivered at the state and local levels.

The enumerated powers of the federal government to spend money are defined in the Constitution under Article I, Section 8. These powers include the right to "establish Post Offices and post roads; raise and support Armies; provide and maintain a Navy; declare War . . ." and to conduct a few other activities related mostly to national defense. No matter how long one searches, it is impossible to find in the Constitution any language that authorizes at least 90 percent of the civilian programs that Congress crams into the federal budget today.

The federal government has no authority to pay money to farmers, run the health care industry, impose wage and price controls, give welfare to the poor and unemployed, provide job training, subsidize electricity and telephone service, lend money to businesses and foreign governments, or build parking garages, tennis courts, and swimming pools. The Founders did not create a Department of Commerce, a Department of Education, or a Department of Housing and Urban Development. This was no oversight: They did not believe that government was authorized to establish such agencies.

Recognizing the propensity of governments to expand, and, as Thomas Jefferson put it, for "liberty to yield," the Founders added the Bill of Rights to the Constitution as an extra layer of protection. The government was never supposed to grow so large that it could trample on the liberties of American citizens. The Tenth Amendment to the Constitution states clearly and unambiguously: "The powers not delegated to the United States by the Constitution . . . are reserved to the States respectively, or to the people." In other words, if the Constitution doesn't specifically permit the federal government to do something, then it doesn't have the right to do it.

The original budget of the U.S. government abided by this rule. The very first appropriations bill passed by Congress consisted of one hundred and eleven words—not pages, mind you, *words*. The main expenditures were for the military, including $137,000 for "defraying the expenses" of the Department of War, $190,000 for retiring the debt from the Revolutionary War, and $95,000 for "paying the pensions to invalids." As for domestic activities, $216,000 was appropriated. This is roughly what federal agencies spend in fifteen seconds today.

As constitutional scholar Roger Pilon has documented, even expenditures for the most charitable of purposes were routinely spurned as illegitimate. In 1794, James Madison wrote disapprovingly of a $15,000 appropriation for French refugees: "I cannot undertake to lay my finger on that article of the Constitution which granted a right to Congress of expending, on objects of benevolence, the money of their constituents." This view that Congress should follow the original intent of the Constitution was restated even more forcefully on the floor of the House of Representatives two years later by William Giles of Virginia. Giles condemned a relief measure for fire victims and insisted that it was not the purpose nor the right of Congress to "attend to what generosity and humanity require, but to what the Constitution and their duty require."

In 1827, the famous Davy Crockett was elected to the House of Representatives. During his first term of office, a $10,000 relief bill for the widow of a naval officer was proposed. Colonel Crockett rose in stern opposition and gave the following eloquent and successful rebuttal:

> We must not permit our respect for the dead or our sympathy for the living to lead us into an act of injustice to the balance of the living. I will not attempt to prove that Congress has no power to appropriate this money as an act of charity. Every member upon this floor knows it. We have the right as individuals to give away as much of our own money as we please in charity; but as members of Congress we have no right to appropriate a dollar of the public money.

In a famous incident in 1854, President Franklin Pierce courageously vetoed an extremely popular bill intended to help the mentally ill, saying: "I cannot find any authority in the Constitution for public charity." To approve such spending, he argued, "would be contrary to the letter and the spirit of the Constitution and subversive to the whole theory upon which the Union of these States is founded." Grover Cleveland, the king of the veto, rejected hundreds of congressional spending bills during his two terms as president in the late 1800s, because, as he often wrote: "I can find no warrant for such an appropriation in the Constitution."

Were Jefferson, Madison, Crockett, Pierce, and Cleveland merely hardhearted and uncaring pennypinchers, as their critics have often charged? Were they unsympathetic toward fire victims, the mentally ill, widows, or impoverished refugees? Of course not. They were honor bound to uphold the Constitution. They perceived—we now know correctly—that once the government genie was out of the bottle, it would be impossible to get it back in.

With a few notable exceptions during the nineteenth century, Congress, the president, and the courts remained faithful to the letter and spirit of the Constitution with regard to government spending. As economic historian Robert Higgs noted in *Crisis and Leviathan,* until the twentieth century, "government did little of much consequence or expense" other than running the military. The total expenditures for the federal budget confirm this assessment. Even as late as 1925, the federal government was still spending just 4 percent of national output.

Abandoning Constitutional Protections

Several major turning points in American history mark the reversal of this ethic. The first was the passage in 1913 of the Sixteenth Amendment, which permitted a federal income tax. This was the first major tax that was not levied on a proportional or uniform basis. Hence, it allowed Congress a political free ride: It could provide government benefits to many by imposing a disproportionately heavy tax burden on the wealthy. Prior to enactment of the income tax, Congress's power to spend was held in check by its limited power to tax. Most federal revenues came from tariffs and land sales. Neither source yielded huge sums. The income tax, however, soon became a cash cow for a Congress needing only the feeblest of excuses to spend money.

The second major event that weakened constitutional protections against big government was the ascendancy of Franklin Roosevelt and his New Deal agenda to the White House during the Great Depression. One after another, constitutional safeguards against excessive government were ignored or misinterpreted. Most notable and tragic was the perversion of the "general welfare" clause. Article I, Section 8 of the Constitution says: "The Congress shall have power to lay and collect taxes, duties, imposts, and excises to pay the debts, provide for the common defense, and promote *the general welfare* of the United States." Since the 1930s, the courts have interpreted this phrase to mean that Congress may spend money for any purpose, whether there is an enumerated power of government or not, as long as legislators deem it to be in the general welfare of certain identifiable groups of citizens like minorities, the needy, or the disabled. This *carte blanche* is exactly the opposite of what the Founders intended. The general welfare clause was supposed to limit government's taxing and spending powers to purposes that are in the national interest.

Jefferson had every reason to be concerned that the general welfare clause might be perverted. To clarify its meaning, he wrote in 1798: "Congress has not unlimited powers to provide for the general welfare but only those specifically enumerated." In fact, when some early lawmakers suggested that the general welfare clause gave Congress a generalized spending authority, they were always forcefully rebuked. In 1828, for example, South Carolina Senator William Drayton reminded his peers, "If Congress can determine what constitutes the general welfare and can appropriate money for its advancement, where is the limitation to carrying into execution whatever can be effected by money?"

Exactly.

Nonetheless, by the late nineteenth century, Congress had adopted the occasional practice of enacting spending bills for public charity in the name of "promoting the general welfare." These laws often made a mockery of this clause. In 1884, Senator John Morgan of Alabama stormed to the Senate floor to describe the impact of a relief bill approved by Congress to provide $400,000 of funds for victims of a flood on the Tombigbee River. Morgan lamented:

> The overflow had passed away before the bill passed Congress, and new crops were already growing upon the land. The funds were distributed in the next October and November elections upon the highest points of the sand mountains throughout a large region where the people wanted what was called "overflow bacon." I cannot get the picture out of my mind. There was the General Welfare of the people invoked and with success, to justify this political fraud; the money was voted and the bacon was bought, and the politicians went around with their greasy hands distributing it to men who cast greasy ballots. And in that way the General Welfare was promoted!

But the real avalanche of such special interest spending did not start until some fifty years later in the midst of the Depression.

In their urgency to spend public relief funds to combat hard times, politicians showed their contempt for constitutional restraints designed to prevent raids on the public purse. "I have no patience whatever with any individual who tries to hide behind the Constitution, when it comes to providing foodstuffs for our citizens," argued New York Representative Hamilton Fish in support of a 1931 hunger relief bill. James O'Conner, a congressman from Louisiana, opined, "I am going to give the Constitution the flexibility . . . as will enable me to vote for any measure I deem of value to the flesh and blood of my day."

Pork-barrel spending began in earnest. In the same year, for instance, Congress introduced an act to provide flood relief to farmers in six affected states. By the time the bill made its way through Congress, farmers in fifteen states became its beneficiaries. One Oklahoma congressman succinctly summarized the new beggar-thy-neighbor spending ethic that had overtaken Capitol Hill: "I do not believe in this pie business, but if we are making a great big pie here . . . then I want to cut it into enough pieces so that Oklahoma will have its piece."

In 1932, Charles Warren, a former assistant attorney general, wrote a popular book titled *Congress as Santa Claus*. "If a law to donate aid to any farmer or cattleman who has had poor crops or lost his cattle comes within the meaning of the phrase 'to provide for the General Welfare of the United States,'" he argued, "why should not similar gifts be made to grocers, shopkeepers, miners, and other businessmen who have made losses through financial depression, or to wage earners out of employment? Why is not their prosperity equally within the purview of the General Welfare?"

Of course, we now know Congress's answer: All of these things are in the "general welfare." This is why we now have unemployment compensation, the Small Business Administration, the Department of Commerce, food stamps, and so on. Of course, all this special interest spending could have been—no, should have been—summarily struck down as unconstitutional. However, the courts have served as a willing co-conspirator in congressional spending schemes.

In a landmark 1936 decision, the Supreme Court inflicted a mortal blow to the Constitution by ruling that the Agricultural

Adjustment Act was constitutional. The Court's interpretation of the spending authority of Congress was frightful and fateful. Its ruling read: "The power of Congress to authorize appropriations of public money for public purposes is not limited by the grants of legislative power found in the Constitution."

James M. Beck, a great American legal scholar and former solicitor general, likened this astounding assault on the Constitution to the *Titanic*'s tragic collision with the iceberg. "After the collision," wrote Beck, "which was hardly felt by the steamer at the time, the great liner seemed to be intact and unhurt, and continued to move. But a death wound had been inflicted under the surface of the water, which poured into the hold of the steamer so swiftly that in a few hours the great ship was sunk."

The New Deal Court essentially told Congress: It doesn't matter what the Constitution says or what limits on government it establishes, you are empowered to spend money on whatever you please. And so Congress does, even though its profligacy has placed the nation in great economic peril.

Other than the Great Depression, by far the most important events that have fostered the growth of government in this century have been the two world wars. Periods of national crisis tend to be times in which normal constitutional restraints are suspended and the nation bands together under government for a national purpose of fighting a common enemy. Yet the recurring lesson of history is that once government has seized new powers, it seldom gives them back after the crisis ends. Surely enough, this phenomenon is one of Parkinson's famous laws of the public sector:

> Taxes (and spending) become heavier in times of war and should diminish, by rights, when the war is over. This is not, however, what happens. Taxes regain their pre-war level. That is because the level of expenditure rises to meet the wartime level of taxation.

In the five years prior to World War I, total federal outlays averaged 2 percent of GDP. In the five years after the war, they averaged 5 percent of GDP. In the years prior to that war the top income tax rate was 7 percent. During the war the tax rate shot up to 70 percent, which was reduced afterward, but only to 24 percent—or more than three times higher than it had originally been.

Government regulations of the private economy also proliferate during times of war and often remain in force afterward. Robert Higgs notes that during World War I, the federal government nationalized the railroads and the telephone lines, requisitioned all ships over 2,500 tons, and regulated food and commodity prices. The Lever Act of 1917 gave the government the power to regulate the price and production of food, fuels, beverages and distilled spirits. It is entirely plausible that, without the war, America would never have suffered through the failed experiment of Prohibition.

World War II was also the genesis of many modern-day government intrusions—which were and still are of dubious constitutionality. These include wage and price controls, conscription (which lasted until the 1970s), rent control in large cities, and, worst of all, federal income tax withholding. In the post-World War II era, Congress has often relied on a war theme to extend its authority into domestic life. Lyndon Johnson launched the modern welfare state in the 1960s when he declared a "war on poverty." In the early 1970s, Richard Nixon imposed across-the-board wage and price controls—the ultimate in government command and control—as a means of winning the "inflation war." In the late 1970s, Jimmy Carter sought to enact a national energy policy with gas rationing and other draconian measures by pleading that the oil crisis had become the "moral equivalent of war."

While government has been the principal beneficiary of national emergency, the principal casualty has been liberty. As Madison warned, "Crisis is the rallying cry of the tyrant." This should give us pause as Congress now sets out to solve the health care crisis, the education crisis, and the crime crisis. To Congress, a crisis is an excuse to expand its domain.

Turning Back the Clock

Shortly before his death, Benjamin Franklin was asked how well the Constitution would survive the test of time. He responded optimistically that "everything appears to promise it will last." Then he added his famous warning, "But in this world nothing is certain but death and taxes." Ironically, the mortal wounds of the Constitution have been inflicted by precisely those who insist that they want to make it "a living document." Yet to argue that we return to the spirit and the true meaning of this living document is to invite scorn, malice, or outright disbelief from modern-day intellectuals.

Those few brave souls (mainly outside the Beltway) who urge that government should be guided by the original intent of the Constitution are always accused of trying to "turn back the clock." But turning back the clock in order to right a grievous wrong is precisely what we ought to do. There is nothing reactionary or backward-looking about dedicating ourselves to the ideas and principles that guided our Founders and formed the bedrock of our free society.

By all means, let's turn back the clock. Who knows? In the process we might even encourage a few Jeffersons and Madisons to run for Congress.

BERNARD H. SIEGAN

Property and Freedom

The United States Constitution was drafted in 1787 and ratified in 1788. It established a government that was unique then and continues to be so today although many nations now subscribe to its special features. Its uniqueness relates to liberty: I believe no constitution in the world more strongly protects liberty.

The principal purpose of a constitution is to establish a government. Government performs three essential functions. First, it makes the laws; second, it executes the laws; and third, it interprets the laws. In England, from which we obtained the legal system that is employed in this country, Parliament possessed the power to perform or control all of these functions. In the late eighteenth century, the House of Commons was the most powerful component of the Parliament. This meant that an elected body largely ruled the nation.

The Framers of our Constitution chose not to follow the English model. They feared unitary rule, whether by a king or an elected body. James Madison, the most important member of the Constitutional Convention of 1787, explained why he and his colleagues rejected unitary rule: "The accumulation of all powers legislative, executive and judiciary, in the same hands, whether of one, a few or many, and whether hereditary, self-appointed or elective, may justly be pronounced the very definition of tyranny." In short, the Framers of our Constitution did not trust any person or group to possess supreme powers in a nation.

They chose to create a government that is divided into three branches. Congress makes the laws; the President executes the laws; and the Supreme Court interprets the laws. No one branch has supreme power. However, each branch exercises certain powers—which we call checks and balances—over the others.

Let us assume that Congress passes a bill that is intended to become a law. This enactment must then be presented to the President for his approval. If he disapproves and vetoes the bill, it will be null and void unless two-thirds of each branch of Congress votes to override the President's veto. The law may then be challenged as unconstitutional, and if the Supreme Court determines it violates the Constitution, it will be null and void.

Each branch has some power over the other branches. The judiciary provides another example of divided government. The President nominates members of the Supreme Court, and the Senate must concur to confirm the appointment. Congress has the power to create federal courts and to regulate the appellate jurisdiction of the Supreme Court. While we are constantly subjected to new laws, I believe that because of the required Constitutional processes, it is more difficult to adopt a law in this country than in any other. This is no accident. It is deliberate. The Framers believed that freedom and not government authority best serves the interests of this country.

The Constitution enumerates the powers of each branch. Article I sets forth the powers of Congress, and Articles II and III specify the powers of the President and Supreme Court. This is far different from the English system in which Parliament has absolute power. Although democracy means government by the people or their elected legislators, the Framers did not believe that a voting majority should be given supreme power. Essentially, they believed that a majority of the electorate should be supreme, except that they should have no power to deprive people of their liberties.

The Constitution thus established a separated and limited government whose powers and functions were set forth in the document. The original Constitution also contained a limited number of protections for individual rights—but not many. It contained no bill of rights, that list of rights immune from the powers of the Congress and the President. After the Constitution was drafted, it was submitted to the states for ratification. To become binding on all thirteen states, it had to be ratified by nine.

In the ratification debates, those opposing ratification based their case largely on the fact that the Constitution did not include a bill of rights. They claimed that without a bill of rights the government would be able to oppress the people and deprive them of the freedoms of speech, press, religion, and property, and essential criminal trial safeguards. The supporters of the Constitution replied that there was no need for a bill of rights because the government had no power to deprive any one of rights. The government, they said, was very limited in power. In the words of Alexander Hamilton, "For why declare that things shall not be done when there is no power to do?"

However, in order to obtain ratification from the required nine states, Madison and the other members of the Constitutional Convention promised they would seek to have the nation adopt a bill of rights if the Constitution were ratified. After ratification, James Madison was elected to Congress from Virginia. In the First Congress, he introduced the series of amendments to the Constitution that would in time, and with changes, become the Bill of Rights. The Bill of Rights protects the rights of speech and the press, assembly, religion, property ownership, and a wide variety of criminal procedures, such as the privilege against self-incrimination, the right to a jury trial, prohibition against double jeopardy, and the right to bail. Eight provisions protect ownership of property.

- The Second Amendment secures the right of the people to keep and bear arms.
- The Third Amendment states that no soldier shall, in time of peace, be quartered in any house without the consent of the owner.
- The Fourth Amendment protects the right of the people to be secure in their persons, houses, papers, and effects, against unreasonable searches and seizures. It also requires that warrants be issued only on probable cause and that they describe the place to be searched and the persons or items to be seized.
- The Fifth Amendment prohibits the government from depriving any person of life, liberty, or property, without due

process of law. It also prohibits the government from taking private property for public use without just compensation.
- The Seventh Amendment requires a jury trial in civil suits where the value in controversy exceeds twenty dollars.
- The Eighth Amendment forbids both excessive bail and excessive fines.

The constitutional guarantees for property rights do not include the use of property for harmful purposes. Nuisances and other seriously injurious and dangerous uses have never been protected under English or American law. This rule is obvious. The Constitution cannot be expected to protect activities that are harmful. However, the Constitution does secure the normal uses of property—the erection of houses, apartments, stores, and factories—that are essential to our welfare.

Why did the Founders of our nation so strongly protect the right of property? First, freedom is an essential part of the human condition. We aspire to improve our lives by working, creating, and producing. It would violate our personal autonomy, dignity, and happiness if government had the power to confiscate the fruits of our labors. Second, freedom cannot exist if government has the power to deprive us of our property. A power over one's property amounts to a power over his will. Government could make us do things we would not otherwise do if it had the power to confiscate our property. Third, freedom enables and encourages people to use their innovative, creative, and productive talents to provide material benefits to society. The advancement and welfare of our nation depends on it.

These ideas are as important today as they were in 1787. Recent world experience loudly and clearly confirms that the nations that protect property are prosperous, while those that do not respect property rights suffer economically. In the late 1980s, communism—the philosophy that rejected and condemned private ownership—collapsed in all eastern European countries, and with it the idea that government could successfully plan and regulate a nation's economy. After the collapse of communism, the Soviet Union separated into fifteen nations and they, along with the other East European nations, began demolishing their collectivist systems and turning to private ownership and enterprise. They sought economic salvation in capitalism. In 1997, most nations of the world agree that their economic viability and welfare demands the recognition and protection of property rights.

During their long reign, communist leaders continuously expressed their intention to provide a better life for their constituents. They imposed every conceivable law toward that end and were ever ready to adopt new regulations "in the public interest." As a result, the communist nations had an abundance of laws, but, it turned out, never enough food, clothing, and shelter. Communism identified the public good with ever greater governmental authority.

By contrast, the countries that secure property and economic rights have produced many more goods and services for the people by following the opposite principle, equating public interest with individual freedom. Capitalist countries rely on individual ingenuity, creativity, and productivity to improve and advance society.

The experience of the nations emerging from communism reveals that the extent of the transition from a communist to a free economy will determine the success of an economy. Consider the economic situation in the Czech Republic and Bulgaria, nations that I have advised on constitutional matters. During the communist period almost all businesses and factories in both countries were owned by the government. As of early 1997, the Czech republic had privatized—transferred to private ownership—80 to 90 percent of its businesses and factories. The amount of privatization in Bulgaria was less than 10 percent. The Czech economy is flourishing; the Bulgarian economy is severely depressed. Bulgaria's hope for survival depends on it transferring the bulk of its commercial firms to private ownership and providing protection for investment and ownership.

The story is the same for all the former communist nations. Those that support capitalism are economically healthy; those that do not are economically sick. The less power government possesses over property and other economic interests, the more likely that its economy will thrive. It is remarkable how wise the Framers were in providing for limited government.

I believe that the Supreme Court has not always faithfully followed the intentions of the Framers of the Constitution. The Framers would probably not be surprised that this has happened because they believed that government was an imperfect institution, no better and no worse than we are. For this reason, they divided and limited government powers.

The Supreme Court is intended to protect our property from the predatory desires that often dominate the Congress and the state legislatures. Fortunately, the Court has in recent years taken a strong turn in this direction.

In 1987, the Supreme Court decided three cases, and since then several more, which showed greater concern for the rights of ownership than had long existed in that powerful tribunal. Until that year, the record of the Supreme Court was not very encouraging to those who believe in property rights. In 1992, the Court decided the case of *Lucas* v. *South Carolina Coastal Council*; in 1994, it decided *Dolan* v. *City of Tigard*. Both opinions illustrate the highly commendable position the Supreme Court has adopted in securing the rights of property.

In 1986, David Lucas paid $975,000 for two oceanfront residential lots in South Carolina; he intended to build two homes similar to those on immediately adjacent lots. At the time of purchase, no state laws prohibited him from building those houses on his land. In 1988, the state legislature passed an act which prohibited Lucas and other owners of land similarly situated from erecting any permanent habitable structures on their lots. The state asserted that building on those lots would create serious environmental harm.

Lucas claimed his property had been confiscated, and a state trial court agreed, awarding him over $1,200,000 in compensation. On appeal, the South Carolina Supreme Court reversed the lower court and held that the state was justified in prohibiting Lucas from building. Therefore he was not entitled to any compensation from the state.

The South Carolina legislature claimed that the proposed construction would cause erosion and destruction of the state's beach and dune system. Moreover, the preservation of the waterfront promoted tourism, increased public access to beaches, and offered an important habitat for plants and animals. The South Carolina Supreme Court deferred to the legislature and accepted these assertions without subjecting them to serious inquiry.

This position was rejected by the U.S. Supreme Court. Writing for the Court, Justice Scalia stated that when all economically viable use of the property is denied, the test of harm is determined by the laws affecting the use of the property when it was purchased. If Lucas's proposed use had been considered a nuisance or near nuisance under the laws of South Carolina at the time of his acquisition, he would have had no cause for complaint since he had never acquired any right to engage in such activity. However, to allow the legislature to deny at its will all economically viable use would violate Lucas's property rights and did require payment of compensation. On remand to the state courts, the South Carolina Supreme Court found under the U.S. Supreme Court's test there was no nuisance basis for denying Lucas the right to build houses on his land.

The state subsequently settled with Lucas for $1.5 million and obtained ownership of the two lots. Lucas may have recovered his monetary outlay but he was denied the proceeds of his investment to build two houses on the property. Thereupon instead of preserving the lots as open space, the State offered the lots for public sale as home sites. Yet when Lucas owned the property the only uses the state authorities were willing to allow him were to picnic, swim, camp in a tent, or live on the property in a movable trailer. The state sold each lot for $392,500 rejecting an offer of $315,000 for one lot from a neighbor who promised to keep it vacant to protect his view. Thus for a relatively small cost, the state could have preserved one of the lots for open space.

The state did adopt a regulation in 1990 after the trial court's decision requiring that the owner remove any structures that flood or become seaward of the dunes in the event of beach erosion. The South Carolina Supreme Court did not consider this regulation in its opinion. Had this restriction been adopted earlier instead of the building ban, Lucas would have much less cause for complaint. State officials have since acknowledged, that inasmuch as the community is gated and a house is between and on either side of the lots, it would not be possible to establish a public park on Lucas's property.

If the houses Lucas contemplated erecting posed dangers to the environment or property, as was alleged, the South Carolina legislature was derelict in not prohibiting such construction when the state became owner of the property. However, if the construction that Lucas proposed did not present such a problem, the legislature was derelict in depriving Lucas of his rights to develop the lots. Indeed, the final outcome in *Lucas* shows how vital it is in a free society for the judiciary to secure owners against arbitrary and capricious legislation.

Dolan v. *City of Tigard* presents another instance of legislative excess. Florence Dolan owned a 71,500 square foot lot in the city of Tigard, Oregon, on which her retail electrical and plumbing supply store was situated. In early 1991, she applied for a permit to replace the structure with one twice the size, but the city refused unless she dedicated about 7,000 square feet of her property to alleviate the drainage and traffic problems that the city said the new store would create. Although she did not plan to build on either parcel, the city wanted Dolan to dedicate to public ownership two portions of her land, one adjacent to an existing floodplain for drainage purposes, and an additional 15-foot strip also adjacent to the flood plain for use as a pedestrian–bicycle pathway. Dolan challenged the City's requirement for the dedication of land as confiscation, but lost before the Oregon Land Use Board of Appeals, the Oregon Court of Appeals, and the Oregon Supreme Court. The case finally reached the U.S. Supreme Court where Dolan obtained a favorable ruling.

The Supreme Court decided that Tigard did not provide evidence justifying the dedications it demanded of Dolan's land. It failed to prove a close connection between conveying the property to the public and the reduction of flooding and traffic congestion problems. As Chief Justice Rehnquist noted, "The City has never said why a public greenway, as opposed to a private one, was required in the interest of flood control."

"[T]he public good," wrote the great English legal commentator, William Blackstone, "is in nothing more essentially interested than the protection of every individual's private rights." Under our Constitution a person should not suffer penalty except for wrongdoing, and the city had shown no good reason for depriving Mrs. Dolan of her property. A majority vote does not justify confiscation. Oliver Wendell Holmes, Jr., an earlier and very famous justice of the Supreme Court, warned against such government propensities: "[A] strong public desire to improve the public condition is not enough to warrant achieving the desire by a shorter cut than the constitutional way of paying for the change."

Dolan is an easy case for those who believe in property rights. In a capitalist society dependent on private investment to achieve public welfare, government should encourage—not impede—private development. Mrs. Dolan's investment will add to the supply of goods and benefit many people.

Without payment of just compensation to the owner, the City of Tigard had no power to acquire any interest in Dolan's land except that which would remedy the drainage and congestion problems created by the proposed construction. Yet two courts and a government agency were willing to approve Tigard's demand to acquire some of Dolan's property without evidence that it was needed for eliminating these problems. This action does not inspire confidence in public officials and agencies, but it is to be expected in the ideological climate that usually permeates zoning and environmental controversies.

The two examples of legislative excesses that I have described are not isolated instances. Regrettably, quite often city councils and state legislatures seek to impose regulation that deprives owners of their property. Only the judiciary stands in the way, and we should be eternally grateful that James Madison and his colleagues inserted provisions in our constitution to protect us from a legislature's greed and avarice.

The major threat to property rights currently comes from environmental groups who seem to exert remarkably strong influence on local and state legislators. These groups continually seek to stop development that poses no danger to public health and safety. Please understand that I consider myself an environmentalist, but I do not seek to halt the construction of homes, stores, and factories because to do so is truly harmful to the environment.

Prohibiting or limiting development will injure the portion of the environment that is unquestionably the most important, that which houses the people and supplies their material needs. For most people, the home is where the major part of life is spent. Its characteristics greatly influence the quality of one's life. Similarly, a comfortable neighborhood and convenience to work and shopping are requisites for a good and pleasurable life. It is not a question whether the land should be used for development or open space. Sufficient land exists to accommodate both. The overwhelming portion of land in the United States is not urbanized. Statistics compiled by the Economics and Statistics Administration of the United States Census Bureau indicate that as of 1992 only about 6 percent of the total surface area of the nation was developed for urban uses (buildings, roads, airports, etc.).

This information should not be a surprise to air travelers who on a trip of almost any length will fly most of the time over areas that have never been developed. The great bulk of land is not suitable for housing; comparatively few people are willing to live in rural and remote areas, not served by roads or utilities. Also, much terrain is unsuitable for urban development. Given the relatively small amount presently in use, there will never be enough urban development to remove open space within relatively short distances of our cities and towns.

It is often contended that this nation has not provided adequately for the physical environment of its people. But how much or what is "enough"? Contrary to this view, the record indicates that the country has in fact done extremely well in this regard. For a nation whose economy is based on private enterprise, the huge extent of government ownership and control of the nation's land is remarkable.

As previously noted, a relatively small portion of our land, probably no more than 6 percent, is developed for urban purposes. Government owns and manages about one-third of the total land in the country, most of which is protected from or unsuitable for development. According to the *1993 Environmental Almanac,* the United States pioneered the idea of national parks and wilderness reserves. As of 1996 the federal government owns 369 national parks, 192 million acres of national forests, 508 wildlife refuges, and 267 million acres of western heritage lands administered by the Bureau of Land Management. National and state parks contain 87 million acres.

In addition, as of 1996, 104 million acres of public lands are restricted to or managed for "wilderness" use. In size, that acreage is larger than the combined total area of Maine, New Hampshire,

Vermont, New York, New Jersey, Maryland, Delaware, and West Virginia. Federal law prohibits the use of autos or other mechanical transport and the installation of roads or any structures in wilderness areas. Millions of acres of productive forest land are included but timber cannot be harvested. Except largely for sections at the perimeters, the bulk of these enormously scenic territories can be enjoyed only by those physically able to walk, hike, or ride mules for very long distances.

Federal protection of wetlands and endangered species limit private ownership in suburban, rural, farming, and undeveloped areas of the country. Accordingly, our nation has preserved or controlled immense amounts of natural terrain and has set aside enormous amounts of land for recreation.

Although a relatively small percentage of the nation's land has been developed for urban purposes, the land that has been developed has served the nation well. Under our Constitution, owners should be permitted and encouraged to use their land as they deem best, subject to the power of government to forbid use when it will cause serious harm.

In 1789, James Madison, later our fourth President, said in the First Congress: "I own myself the friend to a very free system of commerce, and hold it as a truth . . . that if industry and labor are left to their own course, they will generally be directed to those objects which are the most productive, as this is a more certain and direct manner than the wisdom of the most enlightened legislature could point out."

World history confirms the wisdom of these ideas and our Constitution implements them.

LUDWIG VON MISES

The Limits of Property Rights and the Problems of External Costs and External Economies

Property rights as they are circumscribed by laws and protected by courts and the police, are the outgrowth of an age-long evolution. The history of these ages is the record of struggles aiming at the abolition of private property. Again and again despots and popular movements have tried to restrict the rights of private property or to abolish it altogether. These endeavors, it is true, failed. But they have left traces in the ideas determining the legal form and definition of property. The legal concepts of property do not fully take account of the social function of private property. There are certain inadequacies and incongruities which are reflected in the determination of the market phenomena.

Carried through consistently, the right of property would entitle the proprietor to claim all the advantages which the good's employment may generate on the one hand and would burden him with all the disadvantages resulting from its employment on the other hand. Then the proprietor alone would be fully responsible for the outcome. In dealing with his property he would take into account all the expected results of his action, those considered favorable as well as those considered unfavorable. But if some of the consequences of his action are outside of the sphere of the benefits he is entitled to reap and of the drawbacks that are put to

From Ludwig von Mises, *Human Action: A Treatise on Economics,* 4th ed. rev. (Irvington-on-Hudson, NY: Foundation for Economic Education, 1996).

his debit, he will not bother in his planning about *all* the effects of his action. He will disregard those benefits which do not increase his own satisfaction and those costs which do not burden him. His conduct will deviate from the line which it would have followed if the laws were better adjusted to the economic objectives of private ownership. He will embark upon certain projects only because the laws release him from responsibility for some of the costs incurred. He will abstain from other projects merely because the laws prevent him from harvesting all the advantages derivable.

The laws concerning liability and indemnification for damages caused were and still are in some respects deficient. By and large the principle is accepted that everybody is liable to damages which his actions have inflicted upon other people. But there were loopholes left which the legislators were slow to fill. In some cases this tardiness was intentional because the imperfections agreed with the plans of the authorities. When in the past in many countries the owners of factories and railroads were not held liable for the damages which the conduct of their enterprises inflicted on the property and health of neighbors, patrons, employees, and other people through smoke, soot, noise, water pollution, and accidents caused by defective or inappropriate equipment, the idea was that one should not undermine the progress of industrialization and the development of transportation facilities. The same doctrines which prompted and still are prompting many governments to encourage investment in factories and railroads through subsidies, tax exemption, tariffs, and cheap credit were at work in the emergence of a legal state of affairs in which the liability of such enterprises was either formally or practically abated. Later again the opposite tendency began to prevail in many countries and the liability of manufacturers and railroads was increased as against that of other citizens and firms. Here again definite political objectives were operative. Legislators wished to protect the poor, the wage earners, and the peasants against the wealthy entrepreneurs and capitalists.

Whether the proprietor's relief from responsibility for some of the disadvantages resulting from his conduct of affairs is the outcome of a deliberate policy on the part of governments and legislators or whether it is an unintentional effect of the traditional wording of laws, it is at any rate a datum which the actors must take into account. They are faced with the problem of *external costs*. Then some people choose certain modes of want-satisfaction merely on account of the fact that a part of the costs incurred are debited not to them but to other people.

. . . . If land is not owned by anybody, although legal formalism may call it public property, it is utilized without any regard to the disadvantages resulting. Those who are in a position to appropriate to themselves the returns—lumber and game of the forests, fish of the water areas, and mineral deposits of the subsoil—do not bother about the later effects of their mode of exploitation. For them the erosion of the soil, the depletion of the exhaustible resources and other impairments of the future utilization are external costs not entering into their calculation of input and output. They cut down the trees without any regard for fresh shoots or reforestation. In hunting and fishing they do not shrink from methods preventing the repopulation of the hunting and fishing grounds. In the early days of human civilization, when soil of a quality not inferior to that of the utilized pieces was still abundant, people did not find any fault with such predatory methods. When their effects appeared in a decrease in the net returns, the ploughman abandoned his farm and moved to another place. It was only when a country was more densely settled and unoccupied first class land was no longer available for appropriation that people began to consider such predatory methods wasteful. At that time they consolidated the institution of private property in land. They started with arable land and then, step by step, included pastures, forests, and fisheries. The newly settled colonial countries overseas, especially the vast spaces of the United States, whose marvelous agricultural potentialities were almost untouched when the first colonists from Europe arrived, passed through the same stages. Until the last decades of the nineteenth century there was always a geographic zone open to newcomers—the frontier. Neither the existence of the frontier nor its passing was peculiar to America. What characterizes American conditions is the fact that at the time the frontier disappeared ideological and institutional factors impeded the adjustment of the methods of land utilization to the change in the data.

In the central and western areas of continental Europe, where the institution of private property had been rigidly established for many centuries, things were different. There was no question of soil erosion of formerly cultivated land. There was no problem of forest devastation in spite of the fact that the domestic forests had been for ages the only source of lumber for construction and mining and of fuel for heating and for the foundries and furnaces, the potteries and the glass factories. The owners of the forests were impelled to conservation by their own selfish interests. In the most densely inhabited and industrialized areas up to a few years ago between a fifth and a third of the surface was still covered by first-class forests managed according to the methods of scientific forestry.[1]

It is not the task of catallactic theory to elaborate an account of the complex factors that produced modern American land-ownership conditions. Whatever these factors were, they brought about a state of affairs under which a great many farmers and lumber enterprises had reason to consider the disadvantages resulting from the neglect of soil and forest conservation as external costs.[2]

It is true that where a considerable part of the costs incurred are external costs from the point of view of the acting individuals or firms, the economic calculation established by them is manifestly defective and their results deceptive. But this is not the outcome of alleged deficiencies inherent in the system of private ownership of the means of production. It is on the contrary a consequence of loopholes left in this system. It could be removed by a reform of the laws concerning liability for damages inflicted and by rescinding the institutional barriers preventing the full operation of private ownership.

The case of external economies is not simply the inversion of the case of external costs. It has its own domain and character.

If the results of an actor's action benefit not only himself, but also other people, two alternatives are possible:

1. The planning actor considers the advantages which he expects for himself so important that he is prepared to defray all the costs required. The fact that his project also benefits other people will not prevent him from accom-

plishing what promotes his own well-being. When a railroad company erects dikes to protect its tracks against snowslides and avalanches, it also protects the houses on adjacent grounds. But the benefits which its neighbors will derive will not hinder the company from embarking upon an expenditure that it deems expedient.

2. The costs incurred by a project are so great that none of those whom it will benefit is ready to expend them in full. The project can be realized only if a sufficient number of those interested in it share in the costs.

It would hardly be necessary to say more about external economies if it were not for the fact that this phenomenon is entirely misinterpreted in current pseudo-economic literature.

A project P is unprofitable when and because consumers prefer the satisfaction expected from the realization of some other projects to the satisfaction expected from the realization of P. The realization of P would withdraw capital and labor from the realization of some other projects for which the demand of the consumers is more urgent. The layman and the pseudo-economist fail to recognize this fact. They stubbornly refuse to notice the scarcity of the factors of production. As they see it, P could be realized without any cost at all, i.e., without foregoing any other satisfaction. It is merely the wantonness of the profit system that prevents the nation from enjoying gratuitously the pleasures expected from P.

Now, these short-sighted critics go on to say, the absurdity of the profit system becomes especially outrageous if the unprofitability of P is merely due to the fact that the entrepreneur's calculations neglect those advantages of P which for them are external economies. From the point of view of the whole of society such advantages are not external. They benefit at least some members of society and would increase "total welfare." The nonrealization of P is therefore a loss for society. As profit-seeking business, entirely committed to selfishness, declines to embark upon such unprofitable projects, it is the duty of government to fill the gap. Government should either run them as public enterprises or it should subsidize them in order to make them attractive for the private entrepreneur and investor. The subsidies may be granted either directly by money grants from public funds or indirectly by means of tariffs the incidence of which falls upon the buyers of the products.

However, the means which a government needs in order to run a plant at a loss or to subsidize an unprofitable project must be withdrawn either from the taxpayers' spending and investing power or from the loan market. The government has no more ability than individuals to create something out of nothing. What the government spends more, the public spends less. Public works are not accomplished by the miraculous power of a magic wand. They are paid for by funds taken away from the citizens. If the government had not interfered, the citizens would have employed them for the realization of profit-promising projects the realization of which they must omit because their means have been curtailed by the government. For every unprofitable project that is realized by the aid of the government there is a corresponding project the realization of which is neglected merely on account of the government's intervention. Yet this nonrealized project would have been profitable, i.e., it would have employed the scarce means of production in accordance with the most urgent needs of the consumers. From the point of view of the consumers the employment of these means of production for the realization of an unprofitable project is wasteful. It deprives them of satisfactions which they prefer to those which the government-sponsored project can furnish them.

The gullible masses who cannot see beyond the immediate range of their physical eyes are enraptured by the marvelous accomplishments of their rulers. They fail to see that they themselves foot the bill and must consequently renounce many satisfactions which they would have enjoyed if the government had spent less for unprofitable projects. They have not the imagination to think of the possibilities that the government has not allowed to come into existence.[3]

These enthusiasts are still more bewildered if the government's interference enables submarginal producers to continue producing and to stand the competition of more efficient plants, shops, or farms. Here, they say, it is obvious that total production is increased and something is added to the wealth that would not have been produced without the assistance of the authorities. What happens in fact is just the opposite; the magnitude of total production and of total wealth is curtailed. Outfits producing at higher costs are brought into existence or preserved while other outfits producing at lower costs are forced to curtail or to discontinue their production. The consumers are not getting more, but less.

There is, for instance, the very popular idea that it is a good thing for the government to promote the agricultural development of those parts of the country which nature has poorly endowed. Costs of production are higher in these districts than in other areas; it is precisely this fact that qualifies a large part of their soil as submarginal. When unaided by public funds, the farmers tilling these submarginal lands could not stand the competition of the more fertile farms. Agriculture would shrink or fail to develop and the whole area would become a backward part of the country. In full cognizance of this state of affairs profit-seeking business avoids investing in the construction of railroads connecting such inauspicious areas with the centers of consumption. The plight of the farmers is not caused by the fact that they lack transportation facilities. The causation is the other way round; because business realizes that the prospects for these farmers are not propitious, it abstains from investing in railroads which are likely to become unprofitable for lack of a sufficient amount of goods to be shipped. If the government, yielding to the demands of the interested pressure groups, builds the railroad and runs it at a deficit, it certainly benefits the owners of farm land in those poor districts of the country. As a part of the costs that the shipping of their products requires is borne by the treasury, they find it easier to compete with those tilling more fertile land to whom such aid is denied. But the boon of these privileged farmers is paid for by the taxpayers who must provide the funds required to defray the deficit. It affects neither the market price nor the total available supply of agricultural products. It merely makes profitable the operation of farms which hitherto were submarginal and makes other farms, the operation of which was hitherto profitable, submarginal. It shifts production from land requiring lower costs to land requiring higher costs. It does not increase total supply and wealth, it curtails them, as the additional amounts of capital and labor required for the cultivation of high-cost fields instead of low-cost fields are withheld from employments in which they would have made possible the production of some other consumers' goods. The government attains its end of benefiting some parts of the country with what they would have missed, but it produces somewhere else costs which exceed these gains of a privileged group.

Notes

[1]Late in the eighteenth century, European governments began to enact laws aiming at forest conservation. However, it would be a serious blunder to ascribe to these laws any role in the conservation of the forests. Before the middle of the nineteenth century, there was no administrative apparatus available for their enforcement. Besides, the governments of Austria and Prussia—to say nothing of those of the smaller German states—virtually lacked the power to enforce such laws against the aristocratic lords. No civil servant before 1914 would have been bold enough to rouse the anger of a Bohemian or Silesian magnate or a German mediatized *Standesherr*. These princes and counts were spontaneously committed to forest conservation because they felt perfectly safe in the possession of their property and were eager to preserve unabated the source of their revenues and the market price of their estates.

[2]One could as well say that they considered the advantages to be derived from giving care to soil and forest conservation external economies.

[3]Cf. the brilliant analysis of public spending in Henry Hazlitt's book *Economics in One Lesson* (new ed., New York, 1962), 21 ff.

LUDWIG VON MISES

Liberalism and Capitalism

A society in which liberal principles are put into effect is usually called a capitalist society, and the condition of that society, capitalism. Since the economic policy of liberalism has everywhere been only more or less closely approximated in practice, conditions as they are in the world today provide us with but an imperfect idea of the meaning and possible accomplishments of capitalism in full flower. Nevertheless, one is altogether justified in calling our age the age of capitalism, because all that has created the wealth of our time can be traced back to capitalist institutions. It is thanks to those liberal ideas that still remain alive in our society, to what yet survives in it of the capitalist system, that the great mass of our contemporaries can enjoy a standard of living far above that which just a few generations ago was possible only to the rich and especially privileged.

To be sure, in the customary rhetoric of the demagogues these facts are represented quite differently. To listen to them, one would think that all progress in the techniques of production redounds to the exclusive benefit of a favored few, while the masses sink ever more deeply into misery. However, it requires only a moment's reflection to realize that the fruits of all technological and industrial innovations make for an improvement in the satisfaction of the wants of the great masses. All big industries that produce con-

From Ludwig von Mises, *Liberalism in the Classical Traditio*, 3d ed. rev. (Irvington-on-Hudston, NY: Foundation for Economic Education & San Francisco: Cobden Press), 1985.

sumers' goods work directly for their benefit; all industries that produce machines and half-finished products work for them indirectly. The great industrial developments of the last decades, like those of the eighteenth century that are designated by the not altogether happily chosen phrase, "the Industrial Revolution," have resulted, above all, in a better satisfaction of the needs of the masses. The development of the clothing industry, the mechanization of shoe production, and improvements in the processing and distribution of foodstuffs have, by their very nature, benefited the widest public. It is thanks to these industries that the masses today are far better clothed and fed than ever before. However, mass production provides not only for food, shelter, and clothing, but also for other requirements of the multitude. The press serves the masses quite as much as the motion picture industry, and even the theater and similar strongholds of the arts are daily becoming more and more places of mass entertainment. . . .

It hardly occurs to anyone, when he forms his notion of a capitalist, that a social order organized on genuinely liberal principles is so constituted as to leave the entrepreneurs and the capitalists only one way to wealth, viz., by better providing their fellow men with what they themselves think they need. Instead of speaking of capitalism in connection with the prodigious improvement in the standard of living of the masses, antiliberal propaganda mentions capitalism only in referring to those phenomena whose emergence was made possible solely because of the restraints that were imposed upon liberalism. No reference is made to the fact that capitalism has placed a delectable luxury as well as a food, in the form of sugar, at the disposal of the great masses. Capitalism is mentioned in connection with sugar only when the price of sugar in a country is raised above the world market price by a cartel. As if such a development were even conceivable in a social order in which liberal principles were put into effect! In a country with a liberal regime, in which there are no tariffs, cartels capable of driving the price of a commodity above the world market price would be quite unthinkable.

LUDWIG VON MISES

Property

Human society is an association of persons for cooperative action. As against the isolated action of individuals, cooperative action on the basis of the principle of the division of labor has the advantage of greater productivity. If a number of men work in cooperation in accordance with the principle of the division of labor, they will produce (other things being equal) not only as much as the sum of what they would have produced by working as self-sufficient individuals but considerably more. All human civilization is founded on this fact. It is by virtue of the division of labor that man is distinguished from the animals. It is the division of labor that has made feeble man, far inferior to most animals in physical strength, the lord of the earth and the creator of the marvels of technology. In the absence of the division of labor, we would not be in any respect further advanced today than our ancestors of a thousand or ten thousand years ago.

Human labor by itself is not capable of increasing our well-being. In order to be fruitful, it must be applied to the materials and resources of the earth that Nature has placed at our disposal. Land, with all the substances and powers resident within it, and human labor constitute the two factors of production from whose purposeful cooperation proceed all the commodities that serve for the satisfaction of our outer needs. In order to produce, one

From Ludwig von Mises, *Liberalism in the Classical Tradition,* 3d ed. rev. (Irvington-on-Hudson, NY: Foundation for Economic Education & San Francisco: Cobden Press), 1985.

must deploy labor and the material factors of production, including not only the raw materials and resources placed at our disposal by Nature and mostly found in the earth but also the intermediate products already fabricated of these primary natural factors of production by previously performed human labor. In the language of economics we distinguish, accordingly, three factors of production: labor, land, and capital. By land is to be understood everything that Nature places at our disposal in the way of substances and powers on, under, and above the surface of the earth, in the water, and in the air; by capital goods, all the intermediate goods produced from land with the help of human labor that are made to serve further production, such as machines, tools, half-manufactured articles of all kinds, etc.

Now we wish to consider two different systems of human cooperation under the division of labor—one based on private ownership of the means of production, and the other based on communal ownership of the means of production. The latter is called socialism or communism; the former, liberalism or also (ever since it created in the nineteenth century a division of labor encompassing the whole world) capitalism. The liberals maintain that the only workable system of human cooperation in a society based on the division of labor is private ownership of the means of production. They contend that socialism as a completely comprehensive system encompassing all the means of production is unworkable and that the application of the socialist principle to a part of the means of production, though not, of course, impossible, leads to a reduction in the productivity of labor, so that, far from creating greater wealth, it must, on the contrary, have the effect of diminishing wealth.

The program of liberalism, therefore, if condensed into a single word, would have to read: property, that is, private ownership of the means of production (for in regard to commodities ready for consumption, private ownership is a matter of course and is not disputed even by the socialists and communists). All the other demands of liberalism result from this fundamental demand.

. . . . All those in positions of political power, all governments, all kings, and all republican authorities have always looked askance at private property. There is an inherent tendency in all governmental power to recognize no restraints on its operation and to extend the sphere of its dominion as much as possible. To control everything, to leave no room for anything to happen of its own accord without the interference of the authorities—this is the goal for which every ruler secretly strives. If only private property did not stand in the way! Private property creates for the individual a sphere in which he is free of the state. It sets limits to the operation of the authoritarian will. It allows other forces to arise side by side with and in opposition to political power. It thus becomes the basis of all those activities that are free from violent interference on the part of the state. It is the soil in which the seeds of freedom are nurtured and in which the autonomy of the individual and ultimately all intellectual and material progress are rooted. In this sense, it has even been called the fundamental prerequisite for the development of the individual. But it is only with many reservations that the latter formulation can be considered acceptable, because the customary opposition between individual and collectivity, between individualistic and collective ideas and aims, or even between individualistic and universalistic science, is an empty shibboleth.

Thus, there has never been a political power that voluntarily desisted from impeding the free development and operation of the institution of private ownership of the means of production. Governments tolerate private property when they are compelled to do so, but they do not acknowledge it voluntarily in recognition of its necessity. Even liberal politicians, on gaining power, have usually relegated their liberal principles more or less to the background. The tendency to impose oppressive restraints on private property, to abuse political power, and to refuse to respect or recognize any free sphere outside or beyond the dominion of the state is too deeply ingrained in the mentality of those who control the governmental apparatus of compulsion and coercion for them ever to be able to resist it voluntarily. A liberal government is a *contradictio in adjecto*. Governments must be forced into adopting liberalism by the power of the unanimous opinion of the people; that they could voluntarily become liberal is not to be expected.

It is easy to understand what would constrain rulers to recognize the property rights of their subjects in a society composed exclusively of farmers all of whom were equally rich. In such a social order, every attempt to abridge the right to property would immediately meet with the resistance of a united front of all subjects against the government and thus bring about the latter's fall. The situation is essentially different, however, in a society in which there is not only agricultural but also industrial production, and especially where there are big business enterprises involving large-scale investments in industry, mining, and, trade. In such a society, it is quite possible for those in control of the government to take action against private property. In fact, politically there is nothing more advantageous for a government than an attack on property rights, for it is always an easy matter to incite the masses against the owners of land and capital. From time immemorial, therefore, it has been the idea of all absolute monarchs, of all despots and tyrants, to ally themselves with the "people" against the propertied classes. The Second Empire of Louis Napoleon was not the only regime to be founded on the principle of Caesarism. The Prussian authoritarian state of the Hohenzollerns also took up the idea, introduced by Lassalle into German politics during the Prussian constitutional struggle, of winning the masses of workers to the battle against the liberal bourgeoisie by means of a policy of statism and interventionism. This was the basic principle of the "social monarchy" so highly extolled by Schmoller and his school.

In spite of all persecutions, however, the institution of private property has survived. Neither the animosity of all governments, nor the hostile campaign waged against it by writers and moralists and by churches and religions, nor the resentment of the masses—itself deeply rooted in instinctive envy—has availed to abolish it. Every attempt to replace it with some other method of organizing production and distribution has always of itself promptly proved unfeasible to the point of absurdity. People have had to recognize that the institution of private property is indispensable and to revert to it whether they liked it or not.

But for all that, they have still refused to admit that the reason for this return to the institution of free private ownership of the means of production is to be found in the fact that an economic system serving the needs and purposes of man's life in society is, in principle, impracticable except on this foundation. People have been unable to make up their minds to rid themselves of an ideology to which they have become attached, namely, the belief that private property is an evil that cannot, at least for the time being, be dispensed with as long as men have not yet sufficiently evolved ethically. While governments—contrary to their intentions, of course, and to the inherent tendency of every organized center of power—have reconciled themselves to the existence of private property, they have still continued to adhere firmly—not only outwardly, but also in their own thinking—to an ideology hostile to property rights. Indeed, they consider opposition to private property to be correct in principle and any deviation from it on their part to be due solely to their own weakness or to consideration for the interests of powerful groups.